A Celebration of a Capable Kind o' Gal

ELIZABETH "BETTY" ALBRIGHT

A FIRESIDE BOOK Published by Simon & Schuster

Fireside

Rockefeller Center

1230 Avenue of the Americas

New York, NY 10020

Designed by Bonni Leon-Berman

Manufactured in the United States of America

1 3 5 7 9 10 8 6 4 2

Library of Congress Cataloging-in-Publication Data

Albright, Elizabeth.

The Betty book: a celebration of a capable kind o' gal /

Elizabeth Albright.

p.   cm.

1. Women—Conduct of life—Humor.

2. Women—Life skills guides—Humor.

I. Title.

PN6231.W6A48   1997

818'.5407—dc21   96-49989

CIP

ISBN 0-684-83214-3

This **book** belongs

To _____

Acknowledgments

Many thanks to the following betties for their help with this book: David Schwartz, Betsy Lerner, Dan Lane, Larry Dark, and, bettiest of all, Becky Cabaza.

Contents

prefatory note

Once upon a time...

... there was a little girl named Elizabeth. A nice enough name, in general

terms, but by the time she was four, she knew it wasn't her. Too austere, old-

world, queenly. She was stuck with it, however. She asked her parents to call

her "Judy," but they wouldn't budge. "We didn't give you a beautiful name

just to have you change it" was their rationale.

She thought it was hopeless.

Then she talked to Betty and got a new lease on life!

An Encounter with the Ur-Betty

BETTY WAS HER grandparents' Irish housekeeper. She liked her job. Rather than warring with dirt, she *coaxed it* to go away. When she wasn't waxing the floors or dusting the books, she was alphabetizing the spice rack or regrouting the shower tiles. And no matter how dirty the job, she always managed to look fresh and neat. One might say she was the original "fresh-dressed woman"!

One day when Elizabeth was helping Betty put down new shelf paper in all the kitchen cupboards, Betty, perceptive sort that she was, remarked that Elizabeth seemed glum in spite of their cheerful project.

"I hate my name," Elizabeth moaned. "It's putrid, vile, gross."

Betty winced at those words. "No, no, that's not true. Elizabeth is a fine name."

"Oh, that's easy for you to say. You have a cool name. You're a Betty!"

"But Betty is a nickname for Elizabeth," Betty said.

"Jesus, Joseph, and Mary!" Elizabeth exclaimed, an expression she'd learned at Betty's Noxema-scented knee. "I could be a Betty, too!"

"You can, indeed. But just remember, Betty is as Betty does. The name comes with a responsibility."

"Teach me," Elizabeth begged.

"It's simple. It starts up here, in your mind," Betty said, tapping her temple, "and it ends down here, in your hands. Watch the way I approach my tasks. The truth is in the details."

Eureka!

ELIZABETH'S PARENTS AGREED to call her Betty.
And she was happy, and life was good.

An Effective Modus Operandi

IT DIDN'T TAKE Little Betty long to figure out that there were advantages to having a point of view like Big Betty's. Her world was orderly; her vision clear. Nothing ever bothered her, and she always had a solution to every problem that arose, from how to disguise the mysterious stains on the Romulus and Remus wallpaper in the downstairs bathroom to what Little Betty should wear to a slumber party given by a girl from a different school. By following Big Betty's advice and paying attention to the minutiae of everyday existence, Little Betty soon procured a handle on the big picture as well. As it turned out, life did not have to be as unpredictable as it sometimes seemed. There was a way not only to perceive some sense of order in the universe, but to create it. All one had to do was, well, be a BETTY!

Betties, Betties Everywhere

AS LITTLE BETTY grew, she soon discovered that there were other Betties in the world who also appeared to have an extra measure of knowledge about the secret of life. There was Betty from *Archie* comics who led a rather idyllic, uncomplicated teenage existence, as did the Betty on *Father Knows Best*. Betty White, Betty Furness, and Betty Ford were the kind of sturdy, resourceful women who smiled no matter what was going on in their lives, while the enigmatic Betty Crocker made cake and muffin mixes that tasted just as good in the mixing bowl as they did after they were baked. Bette Midler cleverly began her career singing in the bathhouses in downtown New York, where the steam no doubt did as much for her pores as it did for her vocal cords. And, with admirable timing, Betty Friedan meticulously documented *The Feminine Mystique*.

Then there were the unsung Betties, the Betties who were not famous but who'd nevertheless been blessed with a name that set them

apart. Regardless of their race or creed or social class, they performed their daily tasks with a panache and style that made it seem as though they could, if fate called them to do so, fill the shoes of a Barbara Billingsley or a Donna Reed any day. Although they excelled at home economics, their talents extended beyond the household sphere. Anything they touched was as quickly whipped into shape as a meringue topping. Betties adored the kitchen, but they found much to love in the office, the laboratory, and outer space exploration as well.

What's in a Name?

AS I CONTINUED to delve into this phenomenon—yes, I was Little Betty!—I noticed that bettiness was everywhere, in a disproportionate relation to the number of people who were actually named Betty (like *moi!*). In my research, I came across countless women who had all the characteristics of a betty but who happened instead to be called Mary or Sally or Sue. And then there were the men, the Felix Ungers of this world, who proved time and again that bettiness was not a gender-linked phenomenon. All these good folks had the betty sensibility, and they were living the betty life. They just didn't know what to call it.

But Enough about Me, What Do You Think of My Discovery?

AS FOR MYSELF, my intuition about the value of a betty lifestyle was frequently confirmed. Whenever I went astray, things went wrong. For a while, I had a self-destructive fantasy about being a spontaneous, hang-loose type, but a few close calls with spontaneity and things that hung loose served well to disabuse me of that plan. I knew bettiness was the better way, and that was that.

Since then, I have not only tried to live up to betty principles, but also made it my life's work to gather evidence of betty consciousness in our time, and throughout history. This book presents the theory that I have deduced from the facts, as well as provides many interactive opportunities for the reader to hone his or her own betty skills. Did Jean-Paul Sartre ever provide as much old-fashioned fun, not to mention a means to a permanent positive outlook, in any of his books?

Je crois que non.

The Moral

WHEN WE FACE the world with a bettitude (a betty attitude), we find we are able to solve all our problems within the time frame of an average television sitcom. It isn't true that one can't get no satisfaction. One can, and one should. Most of us are betties to some degree. How far you want to go with it is up to you. The possibilities are endless—within reason.

And remember, *de singulis agere veritas,* so speed-read at your own risk.*

Fondly,

Elizabeth "Betty" Albright

Elizabeth "Betty" Albright

* "The truth is in the details."

betty
BOOK

13

are you a betty?

The Betty Quiz

*B*efore we begin our exciting adventure into the happy and fulfilling world of bettiness, let's find out what your BQ (betty quotient) is right now. Circle the letter that best completes the following sentences:

1. Your favorite food is . . .
    a. French
    b. Northern Italian
    c. Japanese
    d. for thought

2. Your favorite insect is . . .
    a. the butterfly
    b. the spider
    c. the Spanish moth
    d. the quilting bee

3. Your favorite patterns are . . .
    a. splashy prints
    b. wild paisleys
    c. giant dots
    d. great checkups

4. You identify with people who . . .
    a. need people
    b. need a personal relationship with God
    c. need money
    d. knead dough

5. Your idea of good fun is . . .
    a. a night out with the boys/girls
    b. night in with the boys/girls
    c. eating, drinking, and being merry
    d. clean

6. You live in a . . .
    a. fieldstone mansion
    b. split-level ranch
    c. fourth-floor walk-up apartment
    d. beltless maxi-pad

7. You like heavy metal . . .
    a. because the lyrics speak to you
    b. because it gives young people an opportunity to collectively vent their rage against a world gone mad
    c. because black T-shirts, motorcycle boots, and pentagrams become you
    d. especially Reynolds Wrap Heavy-Duty Aluminum Foil

8. You would prefer to have a hacking . . .
    a. cough
    b. jacket

9. You exercise so that you can be . . .
    a. healthy
    b. shapely
    c. stronger than dirt

10. If someone hands you a glass in which half the water is gone, you see it as . . .
    a. half empty
    b. half full
    c. unsanitary

11. The most formidable natural phenomenon is . . .
    a. the tornado
    b. the volcano
    c. the tongue twister

12. You would describe your basic personality type as . . .
    a. oral compulsive
    b. anal retentive
    c. All-Tempa Cheer

13. You'll go to the mat . . .
    a. for God and country
    b. for a principle in which you believe
    c. to defend your mate's honor
    d. to do your laundry

14. You like novels . . .
    a. with good, strong plots
    b. that feature intriguing characters
    c. about romantic destinations
    d. of manners

15. Your favorite get-acquainted spot is . . .
    a. a nightclub
    b. the local mall
    c. a museum
    d. Kraft Singles

16. Your favorite symbol of the South is . . .
    a. the Confederate flag
    b. the cotton boll
    c. Dixieland jazz
    d. the Dixie cup

17. You cross your heart and . . .
    a. hope to die
    b. lift and separate

18. Your conception of yourself as a parent is . . .
    a. firm but flexible, depending on the needs of the child
    b. fair and respectful, not condescending
    c. liberal; live and let live
    d. immaculate

19. Your favorite pet is a . . .
    a. dog
    b. cat
    c. hamster
    d. Chia

20. You play it . . .
    a. as it lays
    b. by ear
    c. again, Sam
    d. safe

Are you a betty?

17

Scoring[1]

Ready to add up your points?

Not so fast, Betty!

Don't we all know by now that, valuable as statistics may be, they can also lead one to draw all the wrong conclusions? Surely you have seen examples in your own life of persons who were neither the smartest nor the most deserving, who nevertheless scored the highest on a test? You couldn't help but find this depressing. You resented it. You may have even entertained the gloomy thought that life is unfair.

This is just the kind of thinking that betties try to prevent in themselves and in others. For this reason, rather than confining yourself to the potentially unfair quantification of a point system, you will be graded on your bettitude (your betty attitude) instead. Read the following descriptions and find the one that most closely corresponds to your test-taking behavior:

The Big Betty

• When you saw that you were being asked to take a test, did you sharpen your No. 2 pencils and find a quiet place where you would be undisturbed?

• If you did not know an answer, did you remain calm, go on with the test, and come back to the pesky question later?

• Did you feel you'd done everything you could to prepare for this test?

If so, you are a big betty. You are a walking compendium of Ben Franklin quotes, and your day is made if you receive a free sample of a new laundry detergent in the mail.

The Betty

• Did you sign your name at the top of the test and get off to a good start, only to be distracted by the thought of the powder room sink that needs scrubbing with a nonabrasive cleanser?

[1]Yes, this word has a non-betty connotation (an NBC). If it crossed your mind, skip to the end of this section and rate yourself an Oscar Madison.

- Did you interrupt the test to look up a definition and then read on until you momentarily forgot why you'd turned to the dictionary in the first place?
- Did you waste time checking your hair for split ends while you were mulling over an answer?

You're basically a betty, but your resolve is liable to falter under stress. You need to know you're not alone. Read on.

The Borderline Betty

- Did you circle your answers in ink?
- Did you make one or more cross-outs, permanently defacing this book?
- Did you consider calling a friend to compare answers?

You are a borderline betty. You have several library books in your car that you haven't quite gotten around to returning yet and you've been putting off your semiannual teeth cleaning, but at least you know what you should be doing. With the right isometric exercises, and perhaps a restorative day of beauty at Elizabeth Arden, you can be helped.

The Oscar Madison

- Instead of taking the test, did you skip ahead to see if there were any pictures of naked ladies in this book (see page 61)?
- Did you try to pretend your puppy ate your answers?

You are a barbarian. If you don't change your ways soon, you run the risk of becoming the worst of all social pariahs, the Antibetty.

P.S. The goldfish died ten days ago.

A final note If you circled the last choice for all of the above questions, you are a *bettiot savant*. You'll have no trouble becoming a member of Cleansa, the organization for those whose BQ is Beyond Question. Sharpen your pencils and apply today!

Bettiness Defined

By now you should have some idea of how you rank as a betty. Naturally, you are wondering what all this means. This is not an unreasonable question. You are not an unreasonable person. To the contrary, when you first heard the quote "The unexamined life is not worth living," you felt that little tingle of déjà vu that you often experience when you come across *le mot juste* for one of your own perceptions.

Yet while it's all very well to examine one's life—what could be more interesting?—the betty would be as leery of an excessive tendency toward self-examination as she would of a life that has never been examined at all. Betties subscribed to the golden mean, and therefore think it is best to know just enough, and no more. After all, isn't picking one's brains too thoroughly just about as attractive as picking at any other bodily organ or orifice? And haven't *The Godfather* movies made it clear what happens to people who know too much?

To put it simply: Burberry overcoats are betty. Cement overcoats are not.

With that caveat in mind, bettiness can be defined as the basic human impulse to impose order on the world, to classify, categorize, and tidy up. It is both scientific and artistic, creative and derivative, lofty and mundane. It's perky! It's cozy. It puts on a happy face. And it informs nearly everything we do!

Qualities Betties Admire

charity, chastity, honesty,

integrity, cleanliness, godliness,

neatness, happiness, goodness,

friendliness, punctuality,

Wessonality

Say the Word and You'll Be Free:
A Betty Lexicon

As is the case with every intellectual discipline, bettiness has its own terminology, the mastery of which imparts a pithy accuracy to the user's conversation without the need for a large vocabulary. Betty lingo is short and to the point. By employing betty terms, the user can express herself succinctly without incessantly having to peruse the thesaurus. Below is a list of the principle betty parts of speech and examples of how they may be employed.

(**Note:** Don't be fooled by the relative simplicity with which one can learn this language compared to, say, Chinese. Betty language is uniquely communicative, and its precision quality leaves time for decoupage and stenciling. Can Chinese make that claim?)

Betty

This simple word is tremendously versatile. It can be used as either a noun, an adjective, or a verb.

   a. **As a noun**[2]

      Heloise is a betty.

      Betty is as betty does.

      Was Shirley MacLaine a betty in all her past lives?

   b. **As an adjective**

      Don't you just love her betty window treatments?

      Don't worry, be betty.

      Are those betty Beatles ever going to get back together (see page 172)?

   c. **As a verb**

      On my day off I like to relax and betty around the house.

      Will you please betty up the sink after you finish shaving?

      To betty or not to betty: that is the question.

[2]In the film *Clueless*, the term *betty* is used in a slightly different sense than we are defining it here. Apparently it is sweeping the country as a synonym for "foxy," or "a babe," or even "groovy." We accept the compliment, but, as betties, feel more comfortable adhering to the primary definition.

Bettify.

To improve, redo, or renovate in accord with betty principles.

Martha Stewart did a great job bettifying the White House for Christmas.

By bettifying our kitchen, we increased the value of our house.

Bettification.

1. beautification 2. improvement 3. self-help

A "day of beauty" at Elizabeth Arden is often a quick means to bettification.

Bettitude.

A betty attitude.

His deportment has improved, but his bettitude toward team sports remains ambivalent.

When you finished the quiz at the beginning of this book, you were rated on your bettitude.

Bett.

A nickname and term of endearment.

Hey, Bett, how would you like to go to the Rockefeller Center Christmas Spectacular with me this weekend?

Bête Noire.

A betty of African ancestry.

Whitney Houston is a big bête noire.

Now it's your turn. Try writing a few sentences in the space below using each of these vocabulary words. Chances are you'll find you prefer some more than others, but don't let that worry you. It's very betty to have favorites.

Are you a betty?

Bettifying Existing Names and Words

In order to emphasize the betty essence of a person or a thing, rather than merely grafting on a betty term as a modifier, it is sometimes useful simply to inject *betty* into the name or word itself.

The most efficient way to do this is to substitute the name Betty for part of a person's name. For example, let's say that you have a desire to express the opinion that Andy Warhol was a betty, because of his ability to see the universe in a bottle, his development of a personal uniform, and his devotion to the notion of collectibles. Instead of going into such a long-winded explanation, however, you can convey the same meaning merely by deleting the name Andy and replacing it with Betty.

Andy Warhol = Betty Warhol

Similarly, Barbara Walters becomes Betty Walters, Billy Joel becomes Betty Joel, and so on. This technique waxes most effective when you can make it rhyme.

John Paul Getty = Betty Getty

Helen Reddy = Betty Reddy

Lawrence Ferlinghetti = Betty Ferlinghetti

Middle names, being a naturally betty bit of nomenclature, readily lend themselves to transformation.

Ralph Betty Emerson

Sally Betty Raphael

Ali Betty Khan

Bret Betty Ellis[3]

The final technique that bears discussion is more advanced yet is worth mastering for its subtlety. It involves the deletion of the sound-alike syllable in a word or name and replacing it with . . . have you guessed?

David Betterman

Connbetticut

betticure

bettitude

Bettman and Robin

et bettera, et bettera, et bettera

[3]Why is this man a betty? We think there's a method to his madness, and that his exposure of various perversities that exist in our society is really a plea for a bettier future.

Word Combining

Words that aren't betty in and of themselves may take on quite a different meaning when combined with each other. Below are two lists of words that if combined properly, become betty. Draw neat lines between the two columns to make it happen.

spice	toe
garbage	pin
high	shears
lemon	holder
dumb	boy
rolling	throb
tip	disposal
grape	rack
heart	pledge
pot	waiter

Answers: spice rack, garbage disposal, highboy, Lemon Pledge, dumbwaiter, rolling pin, tiptoe, grape shears, heartthrob, pot rack.

We Have Seen the Betties
and They Are Us

Now you have a new identity and a new language. Don't you feel great?

Isn't this an even better morale booster than a messy face-lift or a smelly oil change?

And this is just the beginning.

To commemorate this transformation, take time now to make a few notes for yourself. Not only will these be fun for you to look back on someday when bettiness has become old hat, but think how much fun your descendants will have reading about your betty beginnings! What bettier heritage could you pass along?

When did you first know you were a betty? _____

_____

_____

_____

What is your earliest betty memory? _____

_____

_____

_____

What is the bettiest thing you've ever done? _____

_____

_____

_____

Are you a betty?

27

What is your most salient betty trait? _____

_____

_____

_____

Which betty part of speech are you most likely to use on a daily

basis? _____

_____

_____

_____

Describe your favorite betty fantasy. _____

_____

_____

_____

What would be a perfect betty day for you? _____

_____

_____

_____

What part of your house could use some bettying right now? _____

_____

_____

Ditto your life? _____

_____

_____

The **betty** BOOK

Write plans to accomplish these bettifications. _____

_____

_____

_____

_____

Record your personal betty beliefs. _____

_____

_____

_____

_____

Who are your favorite betty celebrities? _____

_____

_____

_____

How do you think an awareness of bettiness will enrich your life

from now on? _____

_____

_____

_____

Prominent Betties with the Name Betty

This is a very strict list, and therefore does not include the many Elizabeths who qualify. (See the footnote on Elizabeth Dole on page 33.) But if we betties can't be purists, who can?

Betty White

Betty Furness

Betty Crocker

Betty Ford

Betty Boop

Betty Buckley

Lauren "Betty" Bacall

Bettie Paige

Betty Ruble

Betty Cooper from *Archie* comics

Betty Thomas

Betty Grable

Betty Hutton

*B*elow are some lesser-known betties who popularized the name through their work on or for the silver screen in days gone by:

Betty Blythe

Betty Balfour

Betty E. Box

Betty Bronson

Betty Comden

Betty Compson

Betty Ann Davies

Betty Field

Betty Garrett

Betty McDowall

Betty Jane Rhodes

Betty Stockfield

A Betty by Any Other Name Would Be as Neat

These betties had parents with their own little ideas about nice names for their daughters, but they needn't have bothered. These are all classic betties, no matter what else they're called.

Margaret Thatcher

Naomi Judd

Carol Burnett

Shelley Long

Kathie Lee Gifford

Brooke Shields

Kellie Martin

Katie Couric

Hayley Mills

Sandra Dee

Tracy Nelson

Lori Loughlin

Tipper Gore

Babe[4]

Doris Day

Grace Kelly

Annette Funicello

Paula Zahn

Marie Osmond

Julie Andrews

Martha Stewart

Laura Ashley

Elizabeth Dole[5]

Oprah Winfrey

Shirley Temple

Judith Martin

[4]A nice, clean, positive pig.

[5]Although she no longer answers to it, her nickname used to be Liddy, which is just one of the many nicknames for Elizabeth. Others include, in alphaBETTYcall order: Bess, Bessie, Bet, Beth, Betsy, Bette, Bettina, Betty, Elisa, Eliza, Libby, Lilibet, Lisa, Liza, Lizbeth, Lizette, Lizzie, Lizzy, Tetsy, Tetty. Lots of these gals go back to Elizabeth later in life, but Betties rarely do. Elizabeth Dole's parents could have saved her a lot of heartache if they'd just cut to the chase in the first place and gone with Betty. Let that be a lesson!

Are you a
betty?

Is That Billy Really a Betty?

Although women are often more immediately identified as betties, the qualities that earn them this characterization are by no means strictly gender based. Men can be, and often are, the biggest betties of all! Who epitomizes the betty persona bettier than Felix Unger? All right, granted he's a fictional character and is therefore subject to accusations of exaggeration when cited as a seminal[6] example,[7] but what about these real men?

Tommy Tune

Barry Manilow

Mr. Rogers

Billy Graham

Al Roker[8]

Bill Gates

Paul McCartney

Steve Forbes

Al Gore

Dr. Bob Arnot

Chuck Woolery

The Three Tenors

[6]Be careful with this word, Betty. It can get fishy very fast.

[7]Fictional examples abound, actually. Take note of the Tin Man from *The Wizard of Oz;* the character of Danny, played by Bob Saget, on *Full House;* Carlton on *The Fresh Prince of Bel-Air;* Christopher Robin; and Johnny Appleseed.

[8]Also a bête noire.

Donny Osmond

John Tesh

Dr. Dean Ornish

Neil Diamond

Dick Button

Ron Howard

Robbie Benson

Jay Leno

Warren Buffett

William Bennett

Jim Lovell [9]

Boyz II Men

Dick Clark

Shaun Cassidy

Jacques-Yves Cousteau

Mr. Clean

Mr. Bubbles

[9]Astronaut is a betty profession, although being a fighter pilot—a lot of astronauts were once fighter pilots—isn't. Fighter pilots like pushing the envelope, whereas the betty attitude toward envelopes is far more staid. Licking them is bad enough. Pushing them is out of the question.

Your Betty Horoscope

Here's what the stars have in store for you!

 **Aries** (March 21–April 19)

You are on a collision course with one of your fiercest competitors. Make peace before you crash head-on. If you do crash, cracked glass can be temporarily repaired by applying a coat of white shellac on the inside. This also insulates and weatherproofs, and the glass will still be transparent.

Taurus (April 20–May 20)

A family member is on the horns of a dilemma. Do your best to pry him or her off gently, taking care not to let that pesky bull out of your sight. Your hands can be easily cleaned afterward by wetting them with cool water, then rubbing with a tablespoon of granulated sugar.

Gemini (May 21–June 21)

A double pleasure is waiting for you. Indulge with moderation, and celebrate your good fortune with an attractive array of white candles that have been brightened with any cleaner containing ammonia.

🦀 *Cancer* (June 22–July 22)

A tempting offer may turn out to be a trap. Avoid shallow waters, and if you've temporarily misplaced your rubber sink stopper, a plastic coffee can lid works wonders as a handy substitute.

🦁 *Leo* (July 23–August 22)

Be wary of your foolish pride. The lion's share of good things come to those who wait, and those old bar stools will look like new when you cover the seats with decorative bouffant shower caps.

♍ *Virgo* (August 23–September 22)

Once again you will not get past second base, but don't be discouraged. Bettier safe than sorry! Cheer yourself up by painting your room in a warm, bright shade.

⚖ *Libra* (September 23–October 23)

On balance, it should be a good year. Weigh your options carefully, and shine up the tiles beneath your bathroom scale with one-half cup Borax to one-half gallon water.

♏ *Scorpio* (October 24–November 21)

To avoid getting stung, leave no stone unturned, and save your discarded eggshells to use as a nutrient-packed mulch for the plants in your rock garden.

♐ *Sagittarius* (November 22–December 21)

Keeping your eye on the target will help you reach your goal. Meanwhile, keep your pins and needles sharp by storing them in a pin cushion fashioned from a ball of steel wool covered with decorative material!

♑ *Capricorn* (December 22–January 19)

You tend to bite off more than you can chew. Try drinking a glass of cold water ten minutes before each meal.

Aquarius (January 20–February 18)

Do not allow your occupational worries to spill over into your personal life. For perspiration stains, sponge thoroughly with soap and warm water.

Pisces (February 19–March 20)

An associate's proposal seems fishy to you. Trust your instincts, and get rid of fishy odor by adding three tablespoons of ammonia to the dishwater in which you plan to soak your plates, pans, and utensils.

Are you a betty?

Betty Is as Betty Does

Laudability aside, it really isn't quite enough just to be a betty. True betties are doers. Now that we've established who we are, let's move along to examine betties in action. And where does the betty do the most bettying? Turn the page for a peek at the quintessential betty realm. . . .

the betty at home

ome is where the betty is. Home betty home. Our house is a very, very, very betty house. There's no betty place like home. Just the mention of any one of these aphorisms creates a feeling of peace, doesn't it? And who would deny the truth embedded in these simple phrases? No matter what is going on in the county, country, or world at large, everybody has to go somewhere at night, and no one is more determined than the betty to make sure that somewhere is a happy, pretty, neat home. The home is the foundation of betty culture. It's where we live our betty family lives and raise our betty children. The betty believes that if everybody devoted the appropriate amount of time and attention to their home, there'd be no interest in war and other such unpleasantnesses. Who has the energy for killing people when she's battling staph germs in the bathroom?

In this chapter we'll take a look at some of the telltale features of the modern betty home, but first, let's begin where it all began, with an appreciative nod to some aspects of our betty heritage. Relax. Get comfy (without forsaking your good posture, of course). Imagine a time long, long ago, when the earth was a cold place and everyone needed a good mastodon blanket. . . .

> Betty will be at home after
> 500,000 B.C.
> in dwellings everywhere

Cavemen were the first betties. The moment they arranged their firewood in an ascending pile rather than leaving it scattered about the grotto, bettiness was born. It wasn't long before these kinds of simple organizational skills grew in popularity, and as they did, our primitive progenitors soon found themselves expending less time and energy on survival and having more time and energy for hobbies, such as cave painting, gardening, and elementary fashion design. Thereafter, when bands of cave people met with strangers, they were no longer as likely to immediately try to kill them as they had once been, for three reasons:

1. Having already developed an incipient betty predilection for classification, they were more inclined to study the strangers than to obliterate them.

2. They recognized they had a greater chance of gleaning useful information from fellow cave types than from some of the other creatures that inhabited their landscape, such as, say, the persistently unforthcoming mastodon.

3. They learned that killing has its downside, in that one might be killed oneself in the process.

So instead of fighting, our ancient ancestors began to share tips with their neighbors, and to visit each other's caves. (About this time, Betty Rubble helped Wilma Flintstone organize Bedrock's first block party, and an annual summer tradition took hold.)

Anthropologists have conjectured that the concept of table manners was born when a cave child reached for a shank bone across the expanse of a smoldering fire, thereby learning a painful lesson about the advisability of asking that food be passed to him rather than merely grabbing what he wanted. Similarly, linguists have posited the theory that language grew out of the need for cave couples to comment on each other's culinary, decorative, and parenting skills in more precise terms than mere grunts and gestures could convey.

As these examples demonstrate, our primitive ancestors were motivated not only by hunger and thirst, but also by a primal impulse to express the bettiness in themselves and in others. One needs to go no further than one's own hearth to discover this basic truth. Although we couldn't be further from the cave in terms of our habits and accoutrements, if we are honest with ourselves, we will find that our motivations haven't changed so much. We still hunger; we still thirst; we still betty around.

A fun and educational way to bring this point home, as it were, is to make yourself a betty family tree. I had a lot of fun researching my betty past, and I know you will, too. Just remember to accentuate the positive! Even betties have skeletons in their closets, buy why rattle them when you can create an inspirational family tree like the one that follows, which I made for my clan one Christmas? What more could your descendants ask for than an heirloom like this?[10]

---

[10]Money aside. Let's be real.

Elizabeth "Betty"

Restore Lippincott Albright

b. Sandwich, England, 1600

Organized the second, third, fourth, fifth, and sixth
Thanksgivings until everyone got the idea

Restcome

Opened the first bed-and-
breakfast in the colonies

Recompense
m.
Temperance White

Always wore his'n'hers
pearl-gray capes

William

Hoed tough rows like
butter

Experience
B.S.*

(the name says it all)

Bathsheba
B.S.*

(emulated her sister)

Hester

Cultivated a famous white
garden at her house on
Martha's Vineyard

Fester
B.S.*

(kept baked goods in his
bedroom)

*B.S. = Black Sheep

bright's Family Tree

Patience Stern
b. Bath, England, 1605
Swabbed the decks daily during her
Atlantic crossing and taught shipmates
how to prevent scurvy

emembrance
osed America's earliest folk
g, "Churn, Churn, Churn"

Rebecca
Served the first tossed salad in
Massachusetts

Hardy
Gave famous block parties

m.

Happy Parson
Augmented Hardy's burgers with
her special sauce

Joy
A missionary who taught
African children's choirs to
sing "'Tis a Gifte to Be
Simple"

Chester
His eggnog was known throughout
the county

m.

aroline Windsor Ribbons
ever wore pants in her entire life

Bertram
Saved 10 percent of his income
each year starting at age five,
thereby accumulating a nest
egg of millions

Elizabeth "Betty"
Never forgot a friend's birthday,
and author of this book

Bettiness Marches On

As we have seen, the impracticalities of the early prehistoric era led certain cave persons to invent ways of making life easier, not to mention longer. The pendulum of human development has swung back and forth between chaos and bettiness ever since, encompassing all the stages of vital creativity and morbid decline in between. Every historical period can be examined in light of the predominance or dearth of bettiness therein, the amount of bettiness often being the key to an age. For example, a Macy's clearance sale is betty; the Highland Clearances in Scotland were not.

As Stove Top Stuffing is to a Perdue chicken, so bettiness is the stuffing with which all great civilizations are filled. Bettiness built the pyramids and flew us to the moon. It was the genius behind the individual sugar packet and the Post-it Note. Through bettiness, man has harnessed a hostile and indifferent universe and made it as comfortable as the *Brady Bunch* living room. Study the time line to see examples of bettiness throughout history.

A Betty Time Line

120,000–35,000 B.C. Neanderthals make tools, including rudimentary shrimp-cocktail forks.

23,000 B.C. Hunter-gatherers in France make clay statuettes. Children clamor for stone dream houses and miniature fur coats.

5000 B.C. Rice is cultivated along the Yangtze River in China, and the first jar of sun tea is brewed.

2800 B.C. The world's first steak house, "Stonehenge's," is built on the Salisbury Plain.

2500 B.C. Perfectly straight streets are built at Mohenjo-Daro in the Indus Valley.

2300 B.C. The heyday of mummification—and prototype Ace bandages—in Egypt.

700 B.C. Babylonians invent the calendar and begin development of the Filofax.

560–482 B.C. Siddhartha Guatama lives, founds Buddhism, and advocates the Middle Way. (*Betty translation: Moderation in all things.*)

447 B.C. The Parthenon is begun. Features include symmetrical design, high ceilings, and no-wax floors.

A.D. 1–33 Life of Jesus Christ. He sets a new standard for foot washing, and, at the Sermon on the Mount, demonstrates how to stretch a modest amount of food to feed a large number of unexpected guests.

A.D. 105 Paper is invented in China, facilitating the composition of shopping lists and thank-you notes.

A.D. 539 St. Benedict founds a monastery at Monte Cassino and develops his Rule. (*See* "Top Ten Betty Book Titles," page 132.)

A.D. 595 Indian mathematicians use the decimal system. Groups of restaurant diners can now divide their bills to the last ducat.

A.D. 843 Scotland is united, creating space for great golf courses to be built.

A.D. 1209 St. Francis of Assisi founds the Franciscan order and inspires entrepreneurs to begin developing commercial bird foods.

A.D. 1290 Eyeglasses invented in Italy. Eyeglass chains and quilted eyeglass cases soon follow.

A.D. 1455–56 Johannes Gutenberg makes first printing of the Bible. The publishing industry is born! (*See* "A Perfect Fit Every Time," page 106.)

A.D. 1503 Canterbury Cathedral is completed, and the pocket handkerchief comes into general use in polite European society.

A.D. 1509 Peter Heinlein invents the first watch, and Frau Heinlein begins serving dinner promptly at 6:00 P.M.

A.D. 1518 At a banquet in Venice, forks are used for the first time.

A.D. 1545 First European botanical garden planted in Padua, germinating the formation of garden clubs.

A.D. 1588 The first shorthand manual, *An Arte of Shorte, Swifte and Secrete Writing by Character* is published in England.

A.D. 1589 William Lee invents the knitting machine, resulting in mass production of Fair Isle sweaters.

A.D. 1594 Flush toilet invented by the hygiene-minded Sir John Harrington for his house in Bath, England.

A.D. 1615 Vending machines, selling loose tobacco, appear in English taverns. Exact change is required.

A.D. 1629 Charles I bestows a charter on the League of Spectacle Makers.

A.D. 1630 First installation of sash windows, by Inigo Jones at Raynham Hall.

A.D. 1637 Louis XIII sports a waterproof umbrella!

A.D. 1643 Parcel post established in France.

A.D. 1669 Lampposts installed on the streets of Amsterdam.

A.D. 1675 Founding of the Greenwich Observatory in England. Betties everywhere can officially synchronize their watches.

A.D. 1679 The pressure cooker is invented. (*Tip: Don't forget to bring the steam down before opening.*)

A.D. 1697 Ice skates are used in the Netherlands. Can ice dancing be far behind?

A.D. 1740 *Pamela: Or, Virtue Rewarded* by Samuel Richardson, is favorably received by the public. Pamela was a big betty.

A.D. 1745 French courtiers dance the quadrille.

A.D. 1765 Cotton velvet is manufactured in Lancashire. The

bourgeoisie approves, but the masses demand wrinkle-free fabrics.

A.D. 1769 Josiah Wedgwood opens pottery works in Staffordshire. Dinner parties become easier to equip than ever before!

A.D. 1789 George Washington is elected the first president of the United States. Martha wears first inaugural ball gown.

A.D. 1792 The Federal Mint is established in Philadelphia. After-dinner mints are served in Boston.

A.D. 1816 Invention of the stethoscope and the bicycle.

A.D. 1822 Cotton mills begin production in Massachusetts. American betties want wrinkle-free products, too.

A.D. 1837 The first kindergarten is opened in Germany. Children line up in single file.

A.D. 1846 Invention of . . . the sewing machine. Now anyone can whip up a fresh window treatment.

A.D. 1849 . . . the safety pin. Means never having to run right home when you rip a hem.

A.D. 1855 . . . the Bunsen burner. A fondue pot in every home!

A.D. 1870 . . . margarine. Creamy goodness from the vegetable world.

A.D. 1876 . . . the telephone—a hygienic way to reach out and touch someone.

A.D. 1879 . . . the lightbulb. (*Riddle: How many betties does it take to change a lightbulb? One.*)

A.D. 1880 . . . the ballpoint pen. Even the clumsiest can write without ink blots.

A.D. 1887 . . . Esperanto. Betties who subscribe to this idea only have to learn one language to speak with other betties of all nations.

A.D. 1893 . . . the zipper. XYZ!

A.D. 1895 . . . the safety razor.

A.D. 1899 . . . aspirin, allowing doctors to say, "Take two and call me in the morning."

A.D. 1901 . . . the vacuum cleaner. Praise the Lord.

A.D. 1902 President Theodore Roosevelt proposes a "square deal" for all Americans.

A.D. 1909 . . . Bakelite.

A.D. 1917 . . . frozen food.

A.D. 1927 The name Betty reaches its height of popularity. More children are named Betty than Elizabeth. There is a fad for coupling Betty with other names such as Sue, Lou, Ann, Jane, Jo, et bettera.

A.D. 1937 . . . grocery carts.

A.D. 1945 . . . microwave ovens. (*A tip: Never dry your cat here. Or poodle.*)

A.D. 1952 . . . the transistor radio. Classical music, news, and weather available to all, twenty-four hours a day.

A.D. 1955 . . . the hovercraft. *Whee!*

A.D. 1956 . . . FORTRAN. Move over, Esperanto. Please?

A.D. 1958 The creation of NASA. Calling all space-minded betties!

A.D. 1969 Astronaut Neil Armstrong sets foot on the moon while dressed in an atmospherically correct white suit.

A.D. 1970 Congress passes the Occupational Health and Safety Act. Safety first!

A.D. 1974 ABBA wins the Eurovision song contest.

A.D. 1979 . . . the cellular telephone.

A.D. 1981 *Cats* opens in London.

a.d. 1984 Nancy Reagan attacks the nation's drug problem by wearing trim Adolpho suits and just saying no.

A.D. 1995 The Beatles reunite, and through the wonders of modern technology, record two songs with the late John Lennon.

A.D. 1996 Tenth annual Betty Picnic is held in Grants Pass, Oregon, sponsored by a group of gals on the go who call themselves the Betty Club.

A.D. 1997 Publication of *The Betty Book.*

There are many ways of looking at history, but doesn't this one make you feel glad to be alive? Hold onto that positive feeling for a moment while we move on to discuss one of this century's darker episodes. . . .

How Low Can You Go?

Thanks to television and its worldwide proliferation of cute commercials and shiny all-American sitcom families, the post–World War II period has produced the sharpest increase in bettiness in history, with one glaring exception—*the sixties!* Were it not for their unwavering commitment to the value of accurate record-keeping, betties would prefer to forget the sixties altogether. The only saving grace about that messy era as far as the betty is concerned is the fact that the chaos of the times created a backlash that has resulted in a massive resurgence of bettiness ever since. Leave it to the betty to find the good in *anything!*

The following table presents a compilation of sixties items and personalities that were eventually superseded by their betty complements:

BEFORE	AFTER
Endgame	Endust
flower power	Susan Powter
Woodstock	Index stock funds
acid	antacid
tripping	stippling
Jacqueline Kennedy Onassis	Caroline Kennedy Schlossberg
big bang theory	Athletes for Abstinence
free love	free trade
tie-dye	Ty-D-Bol
The Who	who?

Thankfully, those times are gone and, with luck, the memory of them has become the subject of a healthful repressive mechanism, one of the hallmarks of a betty psychology. If they participated in the sixties madness, they can't recall it—although they're positive they didn't inhale. Other people might dwell on those days,[11] but not betties. Dwelling *in* is more their style. They're over it and looking to the future. The millennium is intrinsically betty, with its neat row of zeros following the friendly number two. Let others wish they'd lived in a different epoch. In the future, betties will clean up!

[11]Oliver Stone.

Gimme (Sic) Shelter

*I*n spite of the vagaries of individual self-expression, there are certain threads that bind the warp and woof of the betty household. The following is a list of items commonly found in bettier homes and gardens. Award yourself one sachet for each item found in *your* house.

ALL AROUND THE HOUSE

- a love seat
- sconces
- tilt-out windows for easy cleaning
- antimacassars
- needlepoint or embroidery pillows or wall hangings stating pithy or humorous observations about life
- collections on display, especially antique teacups, netsukes, Lalique, Wedgwood
- a central vacuum system
- prints, especially Norman Rockwell, Hiroshige, Maxfield Parrish
- claw-and-ball feet on furniture or tub
- burglar alarms and hiding places for valuables
- dimmer switches
- special boxes/shelves set aside for holiday decor
- ditto for wrapping paper and ribbons
- closet and drawer organizers
- a sundial
- color-coded keys kept on a rack near the garage
- a magazine and catalog rack
- an impeccably maintained linen closet
- a for-clothes-only cedar closet
- a decorative ceramic basin with matching pitcher
- coasters
- handy sets of rubber gloves in kitchen, bathroom, basement, and garage
- a hamper with a special compartment for lingerie

- a bag full of discarded clothes now used to perform cleaning chores; likewise, a bag full of reinvented items that might have otherwise been discarded by a less creative person
- wicker

  - tried-and-true cleaning products that really do the job
  - satin-covered hangers
  - wooden hangers
  - no wire hangers
- bookplates in all the treasured children's books
- antique doll beds
- hooked rugs
- carefully captioned photograph albums
- an umbrella stand
- state-of-the-art, sightly recycling bins
- a receptacle for the garden hose designed to look like a decorative pot

- protective glides on furniture
- radios
- flashlights in every room
- curtains, swags, valances
- hand towels in the bathrooms
- outdoor motion lights
- a mailbox designed to hold magazines comfortably
- a collection of greeting cards for all occasions
- pinking shears
- an electric pencil sharpener
- a tea set, complete with two pots
- throw pillows
- a birthday calendar
- a piano or mandolin

  - a birdbath
  - Rubbermaid items
  - desks
  - clocks
  - locks

On Coffee Tables

MAGAZINES

Prevention

Consumer Reports

Ladies' Home Journal

Farmer's Almanac

TV Guide

Victoria

Majesty

Cat Fancy

Martha Stewart Living

Southern Living

Garden Design

Country Living

Woman's Day

Family Circle

Entertainment Weekly[12]

CATALOGS

Lillian Vernon

Cuddledown of Maine

Levenger Tools for Serious Readers

Country Curtains

Williams-Sonoma

Cahill & Co.

Hanna Anderson

Spiegel

Spring Hill Step-by-Step Gardens

[12]Betties love their graded rating system. It really lets you know where you stand.

BASIC BOOKS

Physician's Desk Reference
Zip Code Directory
Bartlett's Familiar Quotations
The Letters of E. B. White
the Fanny Farmer cookbooks
The Way Things Work by David MacCauley
Webster's New Collegiate Dictionary
the Bible
Roget's Thesaurus
Hints from Heloise

Happily in the Closet

peds
driving moccasins
Hush Puppies
Coach bags
scarf tubes
Sansabelt pants
dress shields
cummerbunds and ascots
garters (men's)
gaiters
suspenders
rain scarves
jock straps[13]
Dearfoams
robes, robes, robes
bra slips
dickeys

[13]Unseemly to discuss, yet picture where we'd be without them.

Stuff Is the Staff of Life

Virtually all products are betty in the grand scheme of things. The whole idea of making something and selling it stems from the basic betty impulse to organize the universe. Of course, this essential bettiness may be diluted in the particular by the nature of the function the product is designed to perform, as in the case of rat poison, smart missiles, or pornographic films. Yes, humans have a dark side, say no more. But, for the most part, the products we buy are our greatest helpers, and, in some cases, our very best friends. It's especially gratifying when a manufacturer considers the betty sensibility and gives a product a name that is as appealing as the function of the product itself. Favorite betty product names range from the descriptive (Soft Scrub) to the instructive (Spray 'n Wash) to the clever (Lestoil) to the inspiring (Carpet Fresh). The following are a few of the most beloved:[14]

• Baby Gold Bond (a subtle hint at the old gold standard, which betties believe should never have been abandoned)
• Clairol Herbal Essences shampoo (unbeaten as an evocation of the natural world)
• Comet (cheerily evokes the night sky, and reindeers at Christmastime)
• Prell (trills off the tongue and rings a bell)
• Pampers (evokes a betty's deepest goals and longings)
• Metamucil, Senokot, Tavist-D, Ricola, Robitussin, Mylanta, Ramses, calamine lotion (all poetic)
• Vitalis (is vital)
• Selsun Blue, Aquafresh, Tide, Ocean, Crest, Pond's Cold Cream, White Rain Essentials, Lightdays Longs, Alka Seltzer, Pearl Drops (cool breezes and waterfalls)
• Libby's Juicy Juice (how thirst-quenching can you get?)
• Glad Handle Tie, Kellogg's Just Right, Endust, SlimFast, Duracell,

---

[14]There are a number of betty products and items with such unfortunate names that they can't be included in the official list, for example: the pupu platter, Shedd Spread, lazy Susan, gutters, Brother P-Touch, junket, Beech•Nut, Ben-Gay, Stoned Wheat Thins.

Fixodent (need we say more?)
- Boston Conditioning Solution (solutions are always welcome, and one from Boston has that extra pedigree)
- Pert Plus (perky)
- L'Oréal Preference, Clairol Nice 'n Easy (if you're going to color your hair, wouldn't you prefer it to be nice and easy?)
- Phillip's Milk of Magnesia (ambrosia!)
- Scott Tissue (crisp and clean)
- Excedrin, Orudis KT, Cepacol (these sound like they work)
- Queen Helene Mint Julep Mask, Vanilla Fields Cologne (tasty)
- Polident for Partials (wow!)

Of course, there are many more wonderful products out there in consumer-land, and good betties have opinions about them all. Use the following space to note your thoughts about some of *your* favorites!

The Betty Centerfolds

Now, now. The human body is a beautiful thing! Besides, betties love an occasional sampling of cheesecake, especially with a graham cracker crust. The following depictions of the human form and products used for its glorification are in the bettiest of taste, although parents may want to study these examples with their young children in order to explain certain of the more delicate points. Don't be afraid. *This is educational!*

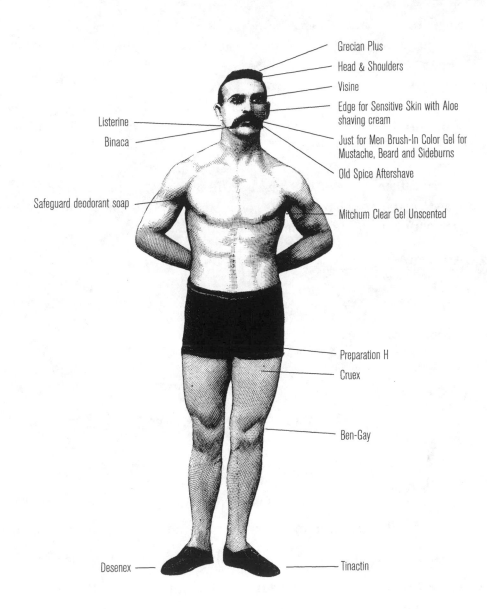

Grecian Plus

Head & Shoulders

Visine

Edge for Sensitive Skin with Aloe
shaving cream

Listerine

Binaca

Just for Men Brush-In Color Gel for
Mustache, Beard and Sideburns

Old Spice Aftershave

Safeguard deodorant soap

Mitchum Clear Gel Unscented

Preparation H

Cruex

Ben-Gay

Desenex

Tinactin

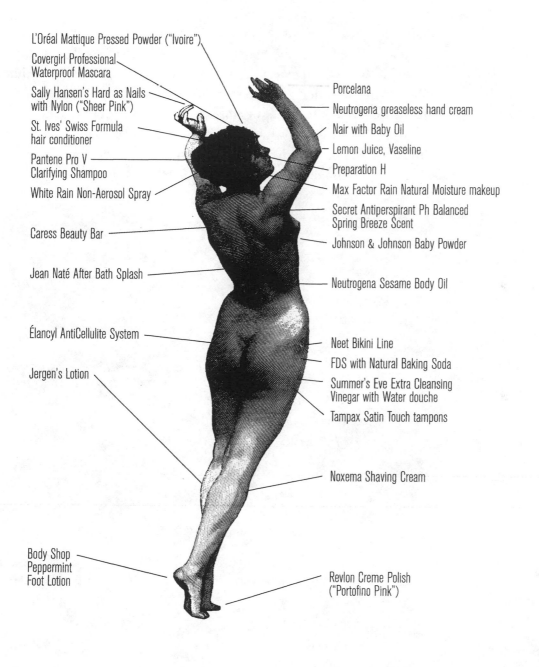

L'Oréal Mattique Pressed Powder ("Ivoire")

Covergirl Professional
Waterproof Mascara

Sally Hansen's Hard as Nails
with Nylon ("Sheer Pink")

St. Ives' Swiss Formula
hair conditioner

Pantene Pro V
Clarifying Shampoo

White Rain Non-Aerosol Spray

Caress Beauty Bar

Jean Naté After Bath Splash

Élancyl AntiCellulite System

Jergen's Lotion

Body Shop
Peppermint
Foot Lotion

Porcelana

Neutrogena greaseless hand cream

Nair with Baby Oil

Lemon Juice, Vaseline

Preparation H

Max Factor Rain Natural Moisture makeup

Secret Antiperspirant Ph Balanced
Spring Breeze Scent

Johnson & Johnson Baby Powder

Neutrogena Sesame Body Oil

Neet Bikini Line

FDS with Natural Baking Soda

Summer's Eve Extra Cleansing
Vinegar with Water douche

Tampax Satin Touch tampons

Noxema Shaving Cream

Revlon Creme Polish
("Portofino Pink")

Betties and Food

The center of the betty home is the kitchen. This is where betties concoct the dishes that fortify them for their busy, friendly, relevant days. They believe they are what they eat (duh!) and therefore expend a lot of time and trouble making sure that what goes in is manifested in attractive ways. They're the people who will order sweetbreads on the basis of the name and then refuse to eat them when they find out what they are. And their finickiness is more often than not borne out by scientific nutritional information. After all, no one ever tried to claim that some scrapple a day keeps the doctor away.

The following comprise the top twenty food groups from which betties are most disposed to choose their nourishment:

1. Anything that sits on a Ritz.

2. Anything in a Crock-Pot.

3. Foods that require expertise or special utensils to eat—fondue (no betty home is complete without a fondue pot, its accompanying one-purpose-only forks, and a six-pack of Sterno), artichokes, lobster, crab.

4. Anything with a French name—vichyssoise, escargots, croque monsieur (or even bettier, croque madame), quiche lorraine, soufflé, blancmange, crème brûlée, canapés, coq au vin, croissants, crepes, petits fours. In fact, though betties are often intimidated by French restaurants, especially if in France itself, they are sticklers for proper pronunciation at home and in lesser, non-French establishments, where they delight in sharing their erudition with the waitresses.

5. Foods that evoke a hint of the exotic within the safety of one's own home—ambrosia, floating island, baked Alaska, gazpacho, Spanish omelet, Jordan almonds. For madcap fun, betties like nothing better than to whip up colorful blender drinks with a South Pacific theme and to accessorize them with miniature paper umbrellas.

6. Foods named after British and Continental countries—English muffins, Belgian waffles, French toast, Welsh rarebit, Turkish taffy, Greek salad, Swedish meatballs, Danish pastry, Scottish shortbread, Irish coffee, German chocolate cake, Polish sausage. These foods make betties feel sophisticated, in spite of the fact that they know full well that many of these dishes are unknown in the countries for which they've been named.

7. Foods commemorating the inventor of the recipe, the place where it was created, or the person for whom it was originally

made—lobster thermidore, beef Wellington, clams casino, oysters Rockefeller, Waldorf salad, fettuccini Alfredo, eggs Benedict, Caesar salad, and cherries jubilee. Betties can't think of a greater tribute than having a dish named after them. (See "Apple Brown Betty" on page 68.)

8. Rustic occupational foods of a bygone era—shepherd's pie, peach cobbler, peasant soup—history and nostalgia both being within the betty's domain.

9. Anything served over toast points—betties all remember eating creamed chipped beef in their grandmothers' kitchens.

10. Casseroles—a foolproof meal in one dish! (See Crock-Pot, above.)

11. Foods that sound wicked and are sinfully delicious—deviled eggs, deviled crab, lobster fra diavalo, devil's food cake, hot tamalè, hot crossed buns. They consider the consumption of these risqué foods an example of their plucky open-mindedness.

12. Tiny little bite-sized foods—hors d'oeuvres, cherry tomatoes, baby corn, sushi, Laughing Cow Cheese, Vienna sausage, all properly grasped between thumb and index finger with idle digits extended.

13. Anything nonalcoholic that utilizes the word *cocktail:* shrimp cocktail, cocktail franks, cocktail olives, fruit cocktail. They associate this word with elegant fun.

14. Eggs your way. (And so many ways there are!)

15. Foods that express the cooking process in their titles—baked potato, broiled lobster, poached salmon, grilled tuna, sautéed onions, stir-fried vegetables, chopped liver, roast chicken, whipped butter, fresh-squeezed orange juice, pressed duck, stewed prunes. Betties like the nod to the cooking technique in the names of these dishes.

16. Jell-O and all molds thereof—sure to add a touch of color to any party.

17. Creamy, smooth desserts—custards, puddings, tapioca, flan—a sensual pleasure that betties can enjoy without shame.

18. Condiments and sauces—the more a food is altered or disguised, the more civilized it seems to a betty.

19. Things that sound like they are derived from animals, but in point of fact are not—bear claws, mousse, hot dogs, Kit-Kat bars, chocolate turtles.

20. Any foodstuff that is new and improved!

Three Squares and Counting . . .

For the betty cook, nothing is more important than having the proper pot, pan, utensil, or appliance for each step of food preparation. Their dream is to own every item in the Williams-Sonoma catalog. Once they acquire a new kitchen item, they have to find the proper place to store it. Betties adore those spacious kitchens with cooking islands in the center and copper pots suspended from a rack overhead. Though few are fortunate enough to have such a setup, this is the standard to which all betties aspire.

They pride themselves on keeping a wide variety of useful and diverse ingredients in stock and are never reduced to knocking on a neighbor's door, measuring cup in hand, because they never run out of anything. Betties buy in quantity and keep ample amounts of dry ingredients in clearly marked canisters on their kitchen shelves or, better yet, in the pantry. Really big betties paste favorite recipes on the canisters, cutting out one extra step between them and a piping hot pan of oat bran muffins. Sugar, brown sugar, honey, salt, pepper, cooking oil, vinegar, butter, eggs, vanilla extract, and baking powder and soda are among the "staples" all betties keep abundantly in stock. And let's not forget the spices! Any betty worth her weight in ounces (dry or fluid) owns a spice rack with matching canisters labeled and arrayed in alphabetical order. They love their sea-

sonings so much that they've been known to seek out recipes that will allow them to use the more obscure ones, such as saffron and coriander.

Betties favor baking over other forms of cooking because of all the measuring involved. Recipes that do not specify exact measurements bewilder them, as do subjective units of measure such as a "pinch." How big a pinch? they wonder nervously. They also do not like recipes that call for ingredients like three "medium-sized" onions. Heavens to betty, what does that mean? They always worry that their onions are too large or too small.

Betties have heard that great chefs cook by taste and add ingredients by eye, but they are not amused by this method of cooking. For them, a recipe is as sacred as the word of God. When a reliable cookbook calls for one and one-third cups of brown sugar, it is not something that they consider open for interpretation. They enjoy watching cooking programs on television featuring such madcap betties as the Galloping Gourmet and Julia Child, but they would never emulate the slapdash style these performers/chefs exemplify. After all, television chefs have people to clean up after them. Betties wash up as they go along. Popping a muffin tin into the oven of a neat-as-a-pin kitchen is half the fun!

Apple Brown Betty

*I*n case you have any itty-bitty doubts left about the correlation between bettiness and the cozy comforts of home, a sampling of this recipe should set you straight. Apple Brown Betty is a staple in functional families all across this great land of ours. Coincidence? Betties think not. Be sure to follow all directions precisely. Happy baking and *bon appétit.*

Serves 6 adults
(between 100 and 175 pounds)

8 medium-sized apples (circumference: at widest point, 9–12 inches; from top to bottom, 8–11 inches), preferably Pippins

¼ cup firmly-packed brown sugar

½ teaspoon cinnamon (if you like more or less, try someone else's recipe)

½ cup all-purpose flour (wasn't that one of the great inventions of the twentieth century?)

¼ teaspoon salt

6 tablespoons butter (no substituting margarine), softened

1. Check your cabinets to see which ingredients you already have and to make sure that shelf paper is in place.

2. Make a list of the ingredients you need. (Some betties simply write what they need as it comes to them. Others write the list in alphabetical order. I prefer to picture the layout of my local supermarket and list the items in order of the aisles where they are kept, as I traverse the store from right to left, then counterclockwise around the perimeter.)

3. Check to see if there is anything else you need and add those items to the list.

4. Peruse your coupon caddy to see if you have coupons for any of the items on your list.

5. Arrange the coupons to correspond to the order on your list.

6. Make sure you have your car keys, your house keys, your driver's license, cash, your Totes supplies (umbrella, runabouts), and a few moist towelettes in case of an accident. Before you leave the house, check to see that all appliances are turned off so you will be free to enjoy your shopping expedition without any nagging worries at the back of your mind.

7. Go to the supermarket and purchase everything on your list. If they are out of anything, particularly an item that is on sale, get a rain check from the manager.

8. While waiting in line at the checkout counter, estimate the amount of money you'll be spending today and make sure that your cash and coupons are accessible so that you don't hold up the line when it comes time to pay. (You used to be able to "guesstimate" on the basis of one dollar per item, but, alas, prices continue to rise. These days it works best to round off to the nearest half-dollar, allowing leeway for the fact that taxes may be levied on some nonfood items.)

9. Pack the cloth grocery bag you have brought from home (plastic is bad for the environment and paper bags cause the demise of far too many trees) while the cashier is tallying your purchases.

10. Pay in exact change.

11. Return home with your purchases, making a special effort to drive carefully and not to think too far ahead to the pleasures of baking that await you.

12. Put all of your purchases away in the proper place.

13. Preheat your self-cleaning oven to 350 degrees. Use an oven thermometer to make sure the temperature is precise. Put on your apron.

14. Peel and core the apples, then slice them into even pieces, about a quarter of an inch wide across the back. (Never pick your knife up by the blade, and always dry it immediately after washing to prevent deterioration.)

15. Combine the dry ingredients and mix thoroughly. This is very important. The more slowly and carefully you perform this step, the less chance you will have of getting any powdery residue on your clothing.

16. Grease your 8-inch round iron skillet with one of the wrappers from a stick of butter that you have previously saved and frozen.

17. Add 5 of the 6 tablespoons of butter to the dry ingredients and mix thoroughly.

18. Alternately layer the apples and the butter/flour/brown sugar/salt/cinnamon mixture in your pan, starting with a layer of apples on the bottom. The same number of slices should be in each of the three layers and exactly one-third of the b/f/bs/s/c mixture should be spread above each layer of apples.

19. Cut the remaining tablespoon of butter into twelve even-sized bits and distribute evenly over the top layer.

20. Place in the oven and immediately set the timer for exactly 20 minutes. Bake loosely covered with aluminum foil. Take the time while you wait for your pie to cook to perform a few extra-special kitchen chores, such as touching up the paint job, defrosting the freezer, polishing the silver, et bettera.

21. Uncover and bake for another 25 minutes.

22. Allow to cool for 20 minutes.

23. Cut into six even pieces (the angle of the cuts between the slices should be exactly 60 degrees) and carefully place each piece on one of your favorite hand-painted 6-inch dessert plates.

24. Serve with a 3-tablespoon scoop of vanilla ice cream placed midway between the point and the rounded back edge of the slice.

25. Enjoy—within limits!

26. Clean all utensils, implements, and your oven (don't forget the screen on your exhaust fan) before you go to bed and make sure all is returned to its proper place.

27. Have sweet, apple-brown-betty dreams. . . .

Seek 'n' Find

With the content of a betty home fresh in your mind, now is a good time to test your BQ by locating and circling all the following words in the puzzle on the page opposite. Remember, words may appear on the vertical, horizontal, or diagonal, spelled backward or forward. Happy hunting!

an apple a day
  keeps the doctor
  away
au gratin
bite size
bobbin
Bon Ami
canister
cardigan
casserole
citronella
cranapple
cupcake
decongest
demitasse
desk set
doily
doughboy
ever ready
Fabergé
fluted
fondue pot
French provincial
Friar Tuck

Girl Scout
gold tone
golf cart
hayride
honest, brave, and
  true
hot toddy
housecoat
itsy-bitsy
Kibbles 'n Bits
lattice
majolica
manicure
mums
napkin ring
nested baskets
nibble
nonstick
nuptial
nutmeg
octagon
paring knife
permanent press
ramekin

rise and shine
rolling pin
saucer
sherry
silent butler
silhouette
a stitch in time
tea cosy
thrifty
Thumbelina
tidy
toaster oven
top hat
trivet
vanilla
willow
Yankee Doodle

```
A C O R K Y B O N I P G N I L L O R I S E A N D S H
U N T H E M A L I C E E L L I O T T D A R K Q U E S
G B A C P A E V E R R E A D Y R R E H S S D C U P C
R E G P A J C F R E N C H P R O V I N C I A L A B C
A H S I P O B I G B E T T Y J F A X W O L L I W I H
T K I B B L E S N B I T S T S E G N O C E D K E L O
I C L T S I E R L A R R Y D A R K I S A N U P T I A
N I H S U C L A V A L U P E R M A N E N T P R E S S
S T O F M A B P D B T V A N I L L A X D B A C R O S
D R U R E L B O N A M I O W X Y Z P Y O U R B U B A
R O E I O X I P L A Y E S R A M I K I N T I E C O R
U N T A L B N I C S O K U T I J B I N G L N U I M G
T E T R D A L L O U T O F R P E O N I P E G R N E U
H L E T B O T C O O L V B E X E N R O L R K T A H P
A L H U O V A T L P I C G E P R L I M E A N D M O A
Z A I C A E M P I R I E F A R S D N S A V I N E V C
E J K K T L O N T C Q U I T C I T G O S O F A X S K
L T O A S T E R O V E N E O I G Y H T E A E E V E K
T C O T K O D O R K P M U M S E O F E U B C V U C B
U U N A I N I S I S I T R E N R E L I D F D A Y O O
T N A G I D R A C T A B C D E F G D H O A R Z A B
H W B C U A Y A N K E E D O O D L E J T K C B L T E
U A F V T L A I S R S A R E L Q P O H N O M T E N R
M D R G I K H E W X S Q X I F Y A B O C Z N S O R E
B L H O J C I D O G A O Z L C D E F T G H I E J R G
A M D Z T D A N E S T E D B A S K E T S K L N M O A
L X Y I E B I T E S I Z E T R I N M O U T B O B B I
I N T P R A X I S V M U N U T M E G D H B R H P R S
N S O P S F O N D U E P O T Q U E E D S I T S Y B I
A O C A T R E P U R D D O U G H B O Y T O C T A G O
```

It Takes Two

What's a home without the people in it? It's just a house, a piece of property, an empty shell. It doesn't become a home until a person moves in, and it gets even homier as the house fills up with a big, happy family. But not too big. Betties are very loyal to the fifties model of the nuclear (oddly, a lot of betties pronounce it "nukular," which is an exception to their general insistence on correct speech) family comprised of male and female married parents and two children, ideally a boy and a girl, with the boy coming first so he can grow up to protect his little sister. Betties love to read books about huge, sprawling families—Laura Ingalls Wilder's Little House books are great favorites—but they rarely go so far as to emulate these massive configurations in their own lives. The prospect of all that laundry is simply too much.

Now, of course, there are all kinds of different families, and as any door-to-door salesman can tell you, it's not uncommon to knock on the door of a betty-looking house only to find a gay or lesbian couple or a betty single parent with adopted children ensconced within. However, like good orthopedic shoes, betties often come in the traditional matching pairs. Ever since Adam and Eve and Noah's Ark, creatures have been doubling up and wandering the world in twos, intuitively under-

standing that the whole is greater than the sum of its parts and that they are more liable to get their money's worth out of second-entrée-50-percent-off coupons if they show up at restaurants as a duo. This only stands to reason, as the idea of a pair is in itself a betty concept, and out of this idea many great betty institutions have arisen and come to dominate society. (Of course, there is a biological explanation for this phenomenon as well, but biology only dictates a moment, whereas bettiness can carry a couple right through to their golden anniversary and beyond.) In a nutshell: Marriage is betty. Divorce is not.

But marriage cannot always work miracles. Princess Diana and Prince Charles were unable to pull off a satisfactory betty union, despite the wedding to end all weddings, the well-appointed palaces, and the hundreds of years of history and tradition to bolster them up. And some couples are able to form a solid betty union without the legal sanction, as in the cases of Tim Robbins and Susan Sarandon, and Goldie Hawn and Kurt Russell. If you feel that getting married or doubling up in some way might serve to bring out the betty in you, by all means go for it. If you are already part of a pair, relax and enjoy. Don't waste time trying to assert your individual identity. Don't look at your situation as being a trap. Fighting it is a waste of energy and will only make you unhappy.

Remember, it is bigger and bettier than both of you.

Betty Couples

Ron & Nancy

Donny & Marie

Hansel & Gretel

two turtle doves

Ozzie & Harriet

Spic & Span

Roy Rogers & Dale Evans

Ted Danson & Mary Steenburgen

Mom & Pop

 soup & sandwich

Mop & Glo

Paul & Joanne

Tweedledum & Tweedledee

Minneapolis–St. Paul

mix & match

Tom Hanks & Rita Wilson

Paul & Linda McCartney

yin & yang

Katie Couric & Bryant Gumbel

Kirk Cameron & Chelsea Noble

David Copperfield & Claudia Schiffer

Oprah Winfrey & Stedman Graham

Shari Lewis & Lamb Chop

John Tesh & Connie Selleca

Crown Prince Naruhito & Princess Masako

Karen Carpenter & Richard Carpenter

Kathie Lee & Frank Gifford*

Tom Cruise & Nicole Kidman

Rodgers & Hammerstein

*In spite of her foray into the miserable netherworld of sweatshops and an eponymous designer label at Wal-Mart, Kathie Lee's bettiness is far-reaching enough to keep her off the Betties Run Amok list (see page 186), at least for now. But please, Kathie Lee, next time don't just wear the fine print—read it, too.

Betty Couples Who Unfortunately Didn't Go the Distance

Billy Joel & Christie Brinkley

Bruce Springsteen & Julianne Phillips

Richard Gere & Cindy Crawford

Gloria Loring & Alan Thicke

Kenneth Branagh & Emma Thompson

Royals, Royals, Royals

Betties and Sex

Did you expect to find a blank page beneath this heading? Did you think it was a joke along the lines of all those old yuks about the shortest book in the library? No, sir! To the betty's way of thinking, those jokes are always in poor taste in that they invariably hinge on some person's or group's inability to function at an acceptable level in some area of endeavor. Betties like a good jest as well as the next person, but they are not liable to find instances of unkindness funny, no matter how clever the presentation. They like knock-knock jokes but eschew ethnic humor, except for the occasional well-timed betty joke. Yes, they can laugh at themselves, and are frequently willing to do so. They appreciate a good comedian and can take large doses of off-color humor from someone who they can tell is a betty at heart—Joan Rivers, for example. Betties are the segment of the population who have enabled the thirty-minute sitcom to become the television format that most consistently dominates the ratings. But we weren't talking about comedy, were we? Somehow, we managed to change the subject. . . .

Betties and Pets

The concept of pets is betty—domestication and all that. Unfortunately, most pets, being animals, are not. Even betty inventions such as the pooper-scooper, cat litters that release a deodorant with every swipe of the paw, sanitary napkins for small animals, and automatic self-feeders have not done away with the inconveniences associated with our feathered and furry friends' alimentary canals. Pets must eat, drink, and eliminate, much to the betty's consternation. For those who simply can't cope, there is the alternative of stuffed animals, with which one knows right up front what one is getting. Stuffed animals are incredibly cute, can be taken anywhere, don't mind being piled up higgledy-piggledy in all kinds of odd and decorative combinations (talk about the lion lying down with the lamb!), and need no surgical modification for any reason whatsoever—although they do tend to lose their ears and other appendages at the hands of young children who have not yet gotten the idea of looking without touching, at which point some sewing may be required.

Yet for some betties, there's no substitute for the real thing. They are willing to live with live creatures of other species in spite of the unpleasantness involved, knowing there are rewards to be had for their troubles. Not the least among these compensations is the incredible world of wonderful products and services that caters to the pet owner. If you think buying a cute Fair Isle sweater for yourself is satisfying, think of the joy to be had by acquiring a miniature version for your dog. What could be more adorable than a tiny ball of fluff clad in a yellow slicker? Then there are the monogrammed pet food bowls, leashes, beds, houses, blankets; commemorative plates; and even decorative gravestones, many of which may all be had for a fraction of the cost of their made-for-human equivalents. What's the annoyance of a bit of litter odor compared to the sheer delight of a rhinestone-studded cat collar?

Some animals are easier to keep than others, however. The following is a compendium of the strong and weak points of some of the most common household pets:

1. **The Gecko** + Rarely seen, this lizard is benign to humans, needs little attention, and will eat up all the stray bugs around the house.
   – Won't keep you warm on a three-dog night, or on any other, for that matter.

2. **The Snake** + Clean, dry, quiet, needs no exercise or companionship, or at least doesn't make these needs known with any of the pawing or moping characteristics of legged creatures. − Live animal feedings, forked tongue displays, ugly surprises when and where you least expect it if the beast gets loose.

3. **The Bird** + Songs, conversation, limited range of movement, colorful. − Droppings difficult to clean, diseases, rapid rigor mortis.

4. **Hamsters, Gerbils, Rabbits** + Cute, cuddly, pellet food clean and fresh smelling, cedar-shaving aroma divine. − Essentially rodents. Hey, why not rat or a squirrel?

5. **The Cat** + Fascinating, beautiful, self-grooming, can be trained to use a toilet. − Litter pan (unless it is of the innovative, self-cleaning variety); needle-sharp teeth and claws; "in heat;" unsightly as road kill; loud, untimely meowing; ruined furniture; fur balls; fur; what are they thinking?

6. **The Dog** + Man's best friend, capable of deep emotional relationships, good exercise companion, can perform in betty dog shows, humorous, can detect drugs and bombs, doesn't mind wearing seasonal costumes (what betty can resist the sight of her beloved poocherino wearing a pair of antlers at Christmas?), trainable. − Drooling, barking, pooping, digging, biting, jumping, humping—well, the list goes on. But despite these drawbacks, betties often choose to share their homes with dogs. *Vive la différence!*

BETTY DOGS

poodle	Scottie
Yorkie	rescued greyhound
Shiba inu	Great Dane
basenji, the barkless dog	Scottish deerhound
miniature pinscher	beagle (betties buy these but get
Shih Tzu	rid of them. But evil Antibetty
West Highland white terrier	animal experimenters love this
	breed for their pliability.)

NON-BETTY DOGS

Labradors	all water-loving breeds
basset hound	pit bull
bulldog	Rottweiler
puli	junkyard

Betties and Children

*I*f ever the betty could be reduced to spouting the rather exasperated saying, *Can't live with 'em, can't live without 'em,* it might well be in reference to the subject of children. Is this any surprise? If the idea of living with a cute little kitten is enough to send the betty into a tizzy, imagine what havoc the specter of a lively toddler might wreak on the serene order of the betty's mind.

Spaghetti flung across the kitchen, white T-shirts smeared with chocolate and peanut butter and jelly, dirty diapers, Legos all over the floor—the betty thinks NOT! But balk though the betty may at the prospect of a child/mess-centered lifestyle, it's not as easy to choose against it as it is with pets. The human race, after all, must propagate itself, and betties consider it their duty to make sure their tidy genes are well represented in the general pool. They take the responsibility for the survival of the fittest personally. No offense to Calvin Klein, but who really knows better how genes should fit than the betty?

So betties suffer the little children to come unto them.

And lo and behold, once the decision is made, they get excited about it. Isn't that just the way? Call it nature, cognitive dissonance, denial, a version of Stockholm syndrome whereby the captive comes to identify with the captor (there are few captivations more compelling than that which exists between parent and child), or whatever, once the betty signs up, she's with the program all the way. Here, as in every other area of the betty's daily life, accessories go a long way toward making for a  happy experience. In those moments of doubt, when betty parents gaze in awe at the maelstrom that has become of their house after even the briefest of play dates on the loveliest of afternoons and wonder what the heck they have done by bringing these beasts into the world, all they have to do to get back on track is to look at little Larry's perky splat mat or little Susie's dotted swiss pinafore. Who could resist? Not the tenderhearted betty. Soon enough, the whole family is singing the Barney cleanup song together and before long the house is neat as a pin again, no harm done, valuable lessons learned along the way. What more could one ask of life than that?

Signposts Pointing to a Betty Future

Babies can't help being a mess, but by the time a child is three or four, the canny parent will be able to spot definite signs that her little darling may well grow up to be a betty.

Does your child…

- prefer lace-up shoes to Velcro and tie them in double knots?
- spend hours obsessively organizing baseball cards?
- learn to read so she can peruse the Pleasant Company's American Girls catalog?
- say prayers without prompting?
- get A's in conduct?
- take a toothbrush to school?
- save allowance for a trip to Disney World?
- wipe her muddy soles on the doormat?
- criticize your driving?
- maintain her own photograph album?
- make countdown calendars for major holidays on the lines of an Advent calendar?
- ask for harp lessons?
- show no interest in owning a pet?
- hate getting sandy/dirty/wet?
- love Mommy and Daddy?
- love life?

If your child exhibits three or more of these traits, you have produced a betty in the making. Now it's up to you to nurture that potential. Start to teach your little angel about the difference between adorable real bunnies and unwanted dust bunnies today!

Betties are different
from you and me.

—F. Betty Fitzgerald

Yes.
They have cleaner closets.

—Betty Hemingway

The betty home is definitely her castle, and when she

has her druthers, there's no place she'd rather be.

But sometimes the betty must go out into the world. The world

is better for it, of course, but for the betty, such venturings

pose a whole new set of challenges. . . .

the betty at large

*H*ello! Welcome to the big wide world, Betty! Of course, it's not as comfortable or controllable as Home Sweet Home, but with any luck,[15] you will be able to blaze the wilderness in a way that makes the world your oyster rather than eating you alive, as it does so many other less self-contained types. Because of your steadiness and reliability, you can fit in just about anywhere. Even in the hippest enclaves, betties are welcome as novelties, if not as living examples of "what we could be if we wanted to." The world depends on betties, and the world knows it. Bettiness makes the world go round. But how, you may ask, does the individual betty maneuver the shark-strewn waters? She applies betty principles to everything she does and she looks at the world through rose-colored glasses that, when not in use, hang from a practical-yet-pretty chain around her neck. . . .

Betiquette

*D*o you wish everyone still used calling cards? Do you gaze wistfully at tea sets in department stores, regretting that you haven't given a tea party since you were eight years old? Do you feel that you could competently hold your own fish fork if thrust into the middle of a Jane Austen or Edith Wharton dinner party?

If you answered yes to any of the above, you have an intuitive grasp of the sensibility necessary for the practice of betiquette. Lucky you!

At first glance, it may seem that there is little difference between betiquette and the more commonplace etiquette. Yet there is a difference, and it is an important one. Etiquette stresses human behavior in social situations, whereas betiquette emphasizes the props. Where etiquette delineates an attitude that can gloss over the details in an awkward situation, betiquette is the sensibility that attends to those details—the principle being that when the details are right, the event will fall into place.

For further illustrations of this principle, we'll turn to an expert. Aunt Betty has been covering betiquette for many years—and, although it would make her blush to hear this said, I think you'll agree that nobody does it bettier!

[15]Betties often speak of luck, but it's really a form of wishful thinking on their part, as they don't believe in it deep down. Instead, they place all their eggs in the baskets of hard work, perseverance, and careful planning. When things come out well, however, they love the dash and pretense of spontaneity in chalking their successes up to "good luck."

Aunt Betty Explains It All

Dear Aunt Betty,

How do I set the table for an informal luncheon for my mothers' group? We are four women with six children under the age of three.

Yours truly,

Frazzled in Fresno

Dear Frazzled,

The proper form for table settings can be found in any good etiquette book. (My personal favorite is *Vogue's Book of Etiquette—A Complete Guide to Traditional Forms and Modern Usage* by Millicent Fenwick. Comb local yard sales for this compendium of good advice!) You can look this information up as well as I can. Where I can best aid you is with your poor self-image. Frazzled is not a gratifying way to feel about oneself. Even the word grates—too close to *frizzy*, *frowsy*, and *floozie* for my taste. If you don't begin to pull yourself together now, your mothers' groups and informal luncheons will leave you feeling more frazzled than ever. Here are a few tips to help whip you into shape.

1. Clean out your linen closet. Setting the table is much more fun when it begins with a thoughtful perusal of an orderly, ironed stack of napkins and tablecloths. Lay fresh shelf paper with a clean, appetizing scent and organize your stacks of sheets and table linens. Beneath each stack, fasten a hand-lettered label—calligraphy looks best—to the edge of the shelf with a smidgeon of easily removable adhesive. That will afford you the freedom of rearranging anytime you conceive of a better plan.

2. Do the same with your silver and glasses. If you have spotting problems on either, make a thorough investigation of cleaning products that will bring them up to snuff.

3. Buy painter's drop cloths and spread them over all your good furniture and your floors before your mothers' group arrives. You can stencil this to

make it look decorative, or just give the children a set of rubber stamps and let them do the job. Remember, betties can tolerate a mess, as long as it is for a good cause and under control.

4. Rethink your birth control method.

5. Move. Fresno would frazzle anyone. How about Santa Barbara?

Dear Aunt Betty,

My daughter and her boyfriend are coming up to visit us for a week at our summer house in Martha's Vineyard. What shall I do about the sleeping arrangements?

Best regards,

A mother-in-law—NOT!

Dear NOT,

Your question raises a perfect opportunity to clear up the difference between etiquette and betiquette. As far as the betty is concerned, your question is moot—assuming, that is, that the sheets on your beds are 100 percent cotton and ironed, and that you take care to put vases of fresh seasonal flowers on the chest of drawers in each room and interesting books on your bedside tables. If your guest rooms look pretty, who cares who sleeps where?

Be sure to leave a can of cleanser and a clean sponge in the bathroom so your visitors can clean the tub after each use. It is within your rights to ask your guests to remove their muddy shoes before they walk through the door. What they do behind a closed one is their own business.

Dear Aunt Betty,

I have been invited to a dinner party and want to make a good impression. What shall I talk about?

Yours truly,

Ms. Foot-in-Mouth Disease

Dear Ms. Foot,

This is a disease for which there is a simple cure. Here it is in a nutshell: SPEAK, BETTY!

You can do this in either of two ways. You can either stick to betty topics of conversation, or you can discuss more general/controversial topics from a betty point of view.

To get you started, here are a few tried-and-true betty topics that should initiate lively discussions. (If they don't, perhaps you shouldn't care so much about impressing this group after all.)

1. vitamins—synthetic or natural? megadoses or the RDA?

2. starch—spray? cube? how often? how much? How does one most effectively communicate one's preferences to the personnel in a Chinese laundry?

3. life insurance—whole-life or term? mutual or profitable? For a real attention grabber, brush up on the topic of actuarial tables, then tell everyone at the table how long they can expect to live.

4. Dear Abby versus Ann Landers—isn't it incredible that two sisters ended up doing the same kind of column? Spin this off into a discussion of siblings in general, although ix-nay on the cest-inay.

5. cake—mixes versus scratch, the eternal debate, eternally compelling.

6. morning talk show personalities—ask if anyone has ever noticed how many newswomen have hair that touches under their chins.

7. skirt lengths—does it really matter? (*Nota bene*—men and women are likely to differ on this point. If the discussion becomes too lively, "skirt" the issue by pulling a quick switcheroo to one of the topics above.)

When it comes to subjects that doesn't seem intrinsically betty, just give it a betty slant. For instance, if the group is talking about whether or not gays should be in the military, you can gently turn the conversation to everything about the military that is betty, such as the wide variety of practical yet spiffy uniforms, the blankets you can bounce a quarter off, the proper method of

folding a flag, et cetera—topics that could conceivably carry one right through dessert. Then you could further point out that gays are some the biggest betties on earth, and what a shame it is to keep such resources confined to dry land. Voilà! You've promoted bettiness and egalitarianism, too. What could be more pleasant?

Dear Aunt Betty,

What part do manners play in betiquette?

Best,

A friend

Dear Friend,

Not knowing any better, a guest at a dinner party drank the contents of a finger bowl. To spare him embarrassment, the hostess did the same. That is good manners.

Not knowing whether or not her guests are clued in to finger bowls, the hostess leaves them out of her party plan altogether. That is betiquette.

In other words, manners are betty, but betiquette puts them in their place.

Thanks, Aunt Betty! We'll do our best to see things through your eyes as we go about our busy days. . . .

The Basic Betiquette Bookshelf

The following books belong in every betty's permanent collection, for easy reference and inspirational reading alike.

Amy Vanderbilt's Etiquette, by Amy Vanderbilt

Emily Post's Etiquette, by Elizabeth L. Post

Crane's Wedding Blue Book, by Steven L. Feinberg

Executive Etiquette in the New Workplace, by Marjabelle Stewart

Don't Slurp Your Food!, by Betty Craig

The Art and Etiquette of Gift Giving, by Dawn Bryan

Amy Vanderbilt's Everyday Etiquette, by Amy Vanderbilt

The Amy Vanderbilt Complete Book of Etiquette, by Nancy Tuckerman and Nancy Duncan

A Book of Common Sense Etiquette, by Eleanor Roosevelt

The Complete Book of Table Setting and Flower Arrangement, by Amelia Hill Leavitt

Miss Manners Rescues Civilization and the Miss Manners oeuvre, by Judith Martin

The New Complete Guide to Executive Manners, by Letitia Baldridge

The Lenox Book of Home Entertaining, by Elizabeth Lawrence

Weddings and the Martha Stewart oeuvre, by Martha Stewart

The Encyclopedia of Etiquette, by Llewellyn Miller

No Bad Dogs, by Barbara Woodhouse

The Origin of Table Manners, by Claude Levi-Strauss

Goops and How to Be Them, by Gelett Burgess

Standard Book of Letter Writing, by Lillian Eichler Watson

Living the Beautiful Life, by Alexandra Stoddard

Beyond Jennifer and Jason, by Linda Rosenkrantz and Pamela Redmond Satran

The All-Purpose Betty Birthday Message

You know how time consuming it can be to browse through rack after rack of birthday greetings in an attempt to find just the right cards for your loved ones. And, despite your best efforts, often as not you end up with something you don't really like. Look what you have to choose from at your local card shop: a drawing of a large aquatic mammal surrounded by candy wrappers . . . a photograph of taxidermied kittens in party dresses . . . a photograph of a handsome young man with distasteful cutouts in the rear of his dungarees. Are any of these really going to communicate affection and respect to your mother? Just how many times do you think you can get away with this sort of nonsense?

The all-purpose betty birthday message will solve your birthday greeting problems permanently. It goes well with any blank card or personal stationery, freeing you forever from having to rely on other people's ideas to express your very private sentiments. Last but not least, it's easy to remember, affording you the option of penning your cards last minute at the post office, if need be (although, of course, it's always preferable to do your correspondence at your leisure and at your desk).

Here it is. Memorize this, and you'll never dread birthdays again!

You're not getting older,
You're getting bettier!

Betty Has a Way to Make Somebody's Day

Birthdays are not the only events that betties commemorate. They like to think of themselves as people for all seasons with cards for all occasions. Open a betty's desk (only after receiving permission to do so, of course) and you'll most likely find a wide array of cards celebrating everything from Valentine's Day to Sukkoth, the Fourth of July to the ides of March. At the beginning of each month, the big betty writes out all her cards for the next four weeks, noting the date on which the card should be mailed in the upper right-hand corner of the envelope where the stamp will eventually be placed. On the appropriate dates, off the cards go, legibly addressed and complete with nine-digit ZIP codes every one.

The following are examples of the betty's arsenal of affectionate messages. After reading through these, take some time to author a few of your own, and to set up an efficient card-dispensing system for your household.

HOPE YOU GET BETTIER SOON!
(get well)

BETTE VOYAGE
(vacation)

ALL BETS ARE ON YOU!
(wedding)

HAPPY ARBOR DAY

You've Got to Line a Pocket or Two: The Betty at Work

The most comfortable place for the betty to spend time outside the Acadian precincts of her own home is the workplace. In many ways the office/job site/factory floor expresses the most distilled essence of bettiness, in that the person and her task are viewed as one, and the environment is set up to make this confluence apparent. To paraphrase Keats, "Work is betty, betty work." The terms are synonymous, redundant, an obvious match. You know this without having to be told. Quick—write down the names of three betties at your workplace.

1. _____

2. _____

3. _____

See how easy? Betties are to the office what cherries are to . . . chocolate-covered cherries! It wouldn't be the same without them. When someone has to work late, or calm a cranky client, or stand all morning over a hot copying machine, who you gonna call? The betty, that's who. They may not be the flashiest workers on the scene, but everyone knows who really gets the job done. But when they are praised for service beyond the call of duty, they are liable to shrug and say, "Someone has to do it."

And they're right.
Someone does.
Thank you, Betty, very much.

Betty, the Proactive Worker Bee

Betties are doers (not to be confused with Dewar's) rather than watchers, especially in the office. You never have to tell a betty that an account needs tending or a contract needs vetting or supplies need ordering. By the time you've thought of it, she already has it under control. To hone your skills on how a betty fulfills an active role in the office world, choose a verb from the list of Margaret's Action Words on page 99 and enter it into one of the blank spaces provided within the following narrative. (And since betties naturally have a way with words, try substituting your own verbs—but avoid doing this exercise with an anti-betty!)

8:45 A.M. Margaret Staples _____ briskly through the front door of the Superior National Bank, _____ to _____ Old Charlie, the bank's longtime and well-loved, if crusty, security guard on her way.

"Good morning, Charlie. I hope you had a healthy, low-fat, thoughtfully planned breakfast this morning," _____ Margaret as she _____ her security badge to her lapel.

"Oh, Ms. Staples, I'm trying. When I'm with you, I always think I'll do it, but when I'm standing in line at McDonald's all by myself . . ." Old Charlie shakes his head.

"You keep trying, Charlie. We want you around here for a long, long time," _____ Margaret.

"And you're the heart and soul of the Superior," says Charlie.

Margaret _____ and _____ for the elevator. At her desk, she _____ her pens, pencils, tape dispenser, note and message pads, millefiori paperweight, ruler, and stamp dispenser with one hand, while with the other she _____ to her PC and _____ her messages. Jeez Louise. There's another e-mail message from her secret admirer. "I want to remove your L'eggs All-Day Summer Lights Suntan support panty hose, your Vanity Fair cotton-crotch panties, your practical yet feminine Olga style #319 blush-colored underwire bra, size 34-C, your lace-edged camisole, and then I want to . . ." Margaret _____ no further. The messages from her secret admirer were becoming uncomfortably intimate. She was on the verge of getting upset when she _____ herself there were lots of ways someone could know what underclothing she wore! The records were no doubt in the Bloomingdale's store computer. Nowadays it was possible to know what anyone bought in the course of a year. She had nothing to _____ about. It wasn't as if this person was stalking her around town. She was tough. She could handle it! But if it happened again, she'd have an obligation to _____ it to security, in case this hacker was homing in on bank secrets as well as e-mail. Someone had to _____ responsibility!

Margaret _____ her appointment book and sees that she is due at a meeting in one minute. No problem! She's prepared. She _____ in the conference room right on the button and _____ a burgundy-colored tooled-leather folder squarely before her on the table.

"Gentlemen," she _____, "it is time for Superior to become supreme, and, finally, after much hard work, I believe we are positioned to do it."

Margaret _____ at her notes while simultaneously _____ out of the corner of her eye to _____ her cohorts' reactions to the challenge she has just _____ into the ring. As always, she's _____ them. But she isn't about to _____ on her laurels. No, success just _____ her on. She's _____ the next portion of her presentation when a young man bursts into the room.

"Help!" he shouts. "The main floor of the bank is being robbed!"

The room erupts tumultuously. "Please, everybody, let's remain calm!" Margaret _____ , good sense coming out of her as if by reflex. She _____ the bank officers to line up single file and _____ them back to her office, where she has a monitor attached to the security cameras on the main floor. She _____ the angle until they can see what's going on. Yikes! A man in a ski mask is waving a gun around. He's also carrying a picket sign that reads, "Margaret Staples—do me or else."

Margaret _____ .

"Who is he?" asks the bank president.

"I don't know, sir." Margaret wants to _____ her hands but _____ her powers of discipline to _____ any overt display of emotion. She's a professional through and through. "I'll go down myself and see if there's anything I can do,"

Margaret _____ . It occurs to her as she _____ down the echoing stairs that this is not the kind of bank offering she imagined she'd be _____ today.

Oh, well.

As she _____ onto the floor, the man recognizes her immediately. She _____ a touching vulnerability steal into his hard, doll-like eyes at the sight of her, and she _____ the happy childhood she feels quite certain he never had.

"Margaret," he whispers.

She _____ her cool until the SWAT team has him safely in custody. Then she _____ him.

"You can still make something of your life," she _____ . "You clearly have good computer skills." She almost _____ he look her up at such time as he might be released from the federal penitentiary, but she _____ that might not be prudent.

He tells her he loves her and wants to *%$# her. Then he's whisked away.

"Good work, Margaret," says the president.

"Whatever it takes, sir," Margaret _____ , and _____ it.

Back at her desk, Margaret _____ her head on her arms and _____ . But only for a moment. There's work to _____ , mergers to _____ , clients to be _____ .

Business must go on. And Margaret Staples _____ her priorities straight.

Margaret's Action Words

walks

pausing

greet

says

clips

encourages

grins

heads

straightens

logs on

peruses

reads

reminded

worry

report

take

checks

arrives

positions

begins

glances

peering

gauge

tossed

wowed

rest

spurs

readying

orders

tells

leads

adjusts

blushes

wring

employs

resist

offers

clambers

floating

steps

sees

mourns

maintains

approaches

urges

suggests

decides

says

means

cradles

weeps

do

make

soothed

has

You Go, Girl!

Before a betty can be an ideal office worker and heroine like Margaret Staples, she has to land the job. The following are examples of résumés and correspondence that have helped several betties do just that:

Betty Q. [for Qute!] Cuddlehuddy

Olde Mill Gate Meadow Lane

Beechwood, Connecticut 45709

Objective: To have a nice job in a clean, safe environment devoid of any known occupational hazards, surrounded by cheerful, friendly workers in an atmosphere of unmitigated support and approval, and unbounded opportunities for advancement based on performance, not looks or favoritism or Q ratings.

Experience

Girl Reporter, Super Duper Station WXYZ, 1995–1997. I did all the reports on people's problems with the world of products for three consecutive years, during which time I successfully trained my hair to touch under my chin. Washed out my stockings and underwear before bed every night . . . well, except for once when I had the Shanghai flu. Won an award for: 75 versus 100 Watts: Is Brighter Better? Learned everyone's name the first day (eighty-four people). Accidentally went home with a company pencil on two separate occasions. Loved my desk.

Girl Public Relations Representative, 1990–1995. Handled several large accounts, including Dan Quayle, Arsenio Hall, the movie *Toys,* Mariah Carey. Found three really good Chanel suits at a thrift shop and had them altered (taken in!). Ordered salad dressing on the side at all meals. Secretly continued watching Dave Letterman.

Girl Teacher, Montessori School, 1988–1989. Did my best, but could not

understand what those children wanted. Discouraged excessive use of finger paints and mud pies as learning tools. Refused to give credence to the idea of Circle Time. What's wrong with rows of desks? Never wore jeans and Birkenstocks, the costume of choice for my colleagues. Maintained my pride. Shaved under my arms. Was fired.

Education

Mt. Holyoke, 1986–1988. Triple major in Music Appreciation, Art History, and Special Education. Kept my virginity until senior year. Class Treasurer.

University of Georgia, 1984–1986. A mistake. Wanted to see a different part of the country, chose Georgia because I felt guilty about Sherman's March to the Sea. Got over it.

Miss Dictor's School for Girls, 1972–1984. Posture Prize; Good Sportsmanship Award; Glee Club.

Miss Priss's Kindergarten, 1971–1972. Everything I ever needed to know I learned here.

Personal Information

Single (for now!)
Languages—Swedish, Finnish, Suissedeutsch, Esperanto
Hobbies—Self-Improvement
Sports—Badminton, Croquet, Synchronized Swimming

This résumé garnered Betty many interviews, after which she always immediately wrote a follow-up thank-you note. The following is a copy of a note she wrote after a particularly promising meeting, during which she modestly but confidently met her interviewer's eye and portrayed competent enthusiasm through her body language. She really wanted to land this baby!

Dear Mrs. Powers,

I'm writing to thank you so incredibly such for the wonderful interview today. It was without a doubt the very best out of all the dozens of interviews I've had in the last few weeks; for the first time in ages, I feel like I really connected with another person. What a relief it is to have that inef-

fable sense of simpatico! Wasn't it amazing that we'd both been to Williamsburg within the past year? Some people are meant to meet!

I would like to reiterate my interest in being the morning hostess on your wonderful program. I'm sure we could work well together, and that I could provide you with some much-needed advice on what to do about that slight whisker problem beneath your chin. In fact, why not a regular segment on hair removal? Something along the lines of hormone therapy versus electrolysis? Gosh, just the idea of doing such innovative programming gives me goose bumps. I think I'd better sign off now and go make some notes.

Thank you again for everything. I can't thank you enough! Thank you, thank you, thank you, thank you, thank you, thank you! Hope to hear from you sooner!

Love,

Betty Cuddlehuddy (the first!)

Betty Cuddlehuddy (the first!)

Luckily for Betty Cuddlehuddy, Mrs. Powers had a good sense of humor! She thought Betty was joking most of the time and recommended her for the job because she believed the morning show could use a sense of humor. Unfortunately, a few weeks later there was a misunderstanding when Mrs. Powers came back from a late meeting and found Betty going through her—Mrs. Powers's—desk drawers. Betty insisted she was just neatening them up and certainly intended no harm, but Mrs. Powers had a different interpretation of the event and soon Betty was out on the trail of a new job again. But with a résumé like hers, hey! There was nothing to worry about.

Here's a résumé composed by a newcomer to the job market. Look at how she manages to turn her everyday experiences into harbingers of valuable skills!

Alma Mater
Boxwood Lane
Susiedale, Delaware

Objective: To put my management skills to use in the fast-paced world of business and finance.

Experience

1965–1991   The best way to describe my life is to say that, both literally and figuratively, I wore many hats in my role as loyal wife, and mother of five active children. Although unsalaried, I have held and excelled at (if I do say so myself!) all the following jobs:

Food Services Manager: Made three nutritious squares a day, plus snacks, for five spirited children and their household pets. Comparison shopped, and always took advantage of sales and coupons. Kept up with fast-breaking nutritional information, switching, for example, from Rice-a-Roni to rice bran.

Fashion Consultant cum Personal Shopper: Color-coordinated and mixed-and-matched wardrobes for a frisky family including five feisty children. Always used sew-in name tags and starch. Resisted the dissolution of rules governing the impropriety of mixing blues with greens, stripes with checks, silver with gold. Someone had to take a stand.

Accountant and Financial Manager: Kept the books and paid all the bills for an inexhaustible family of seven. Wrote neatly with a Rapidograph pen, which, incidentally, never became clogged. Rarely had to use red ink.

Textile Maintenance Supervisor: Performed many wash day miracles, including removing all traces of blood from a white lace skirt. Always separated permanent press from natural fabric clothing belonging to five vigorous children. Never lost a sock!

Interior Environmental Design Manager: Decorated the living and dining

quarters, including efficient closet and attic design, for a peppy family of seven. Can do things with contact paper that make most people weep with envy!

Transportation Coordinator: Ran and serviced a fleet of vehicles for a busy husband and five dynamic offspring. Knowledge of how to change tires and get into a locked car without breaking any windows, not to mention how to cook a gourmet meal on a car engine!

Chief of Sanitation Services: Managed garbage disposal for a bustling family of seven and all their pets! (No kitty-litter odor in the Mater house.)

Psychologist: Listened to the problems of and provided advice for a sprightly group of five vivacious children. Greeted news of homosexuality and various arrests with equanimity and good humor.

Manager of In-House Education Programs: Developed a core curriculum of life studies for five impressionable students while at the same time acting as an adjunct educator to the local public school system.

Health
You name it, what with five children, I've been exposed to it. Why not allow my immunities to work for you?

Hobbies
Created a prize-winning pineapple upside-down cake for the Betty Crocker bake-off. Also completed both business and law schools at night and passed law boards in New York, Illinois, and California.

Alma sent out five hundred résumés to the personnel directors of the *Fortune* 500 companies, whose names and addresses she found in her local library. After not hearing anything for six months, she finally got a note from someone who suggested she stress her hobbies over her experience. She rewrote her résumé, and sure enough, she is working at her dream job as an attorney for General Foods Corporation today!

Famous Betty Business Women

You need look no further for how-to examples than the lives of these successful ladies!

Sara Lee

Laura Ashley

Mary Kay

Mrs. Fields

Donna Karan

Georgette Mosbacher

Betty Crocker

Mrs. Butterworth

Mrs. Dash

Little Debbie

A Perfect Fit Every Time

The following are some of the jobs that suit betties the best:

product tester

census taker

maître d'

concierge

any job that requires a uniform—waitress, cruise ship captain,
doorman, supreme court justice

pretty much anything in publishing—copy editor, circulation manager, art director, editor, proofreader

choreographer

cartographer

landscape architect

interior designer

pastry chef

surgeon general

lady-in-waiting

social secretary

haberdasher

master of ceremonies

motivational speaker

clergyman

curator

coordinator

Chancellor of the Exchequer

grand vizier

Whistle While You Work

To ensure a compatible environment, consider working at one of the following companies:

Microsoft[16]

Procter & Gamble

Condé Nast

Nickelodeon

Staples

Brooks Brothers

Estée Lauder

Crabtree and Evelyn

Colgate-Palmolive

Disney

Avis

Franklin Mint

Bad Company

Betty don't work here:

Acme Meat Packing

Harley-Davidson

Zap Comics

Boone's Farm Winery

Hooters

[16]IBM is even bettier, but how does one get around that name?

Betties and Money

Betties have two basic rules about money:

1. Don't touch your capital.
2. Don't touch your cash.

Betties are firm believers in banks. Unless they are rich enough to have trustworthy financial advisers to handle their investments for them (Father knows bettiest), they tend to keep their money at a solid banking institution. Solidity is determined by the following criteria:

1. Is it an old institution? (Brick, marble, and portraits of past presidents wearing powdered wigs provide immediate credibility.)
2. Does it have a good Christmas Club? (It must.)
3. Does the person in charge of the safety deposit boxes wear gloves? (He simply has to!)
4. Are photographs of armed, dangerous bank robbers prominently displayed on the premises? (Run, betty, run!)
5. Do the loan officers have dandruff? (This does not necessarily prevent a betty from becoming a customer at the offender's bank. The betty may well open an account, establish a relationship with the afflicted one, and then, when the time is right, offer a few carefully chosen words of advice.)
6. Does the bank have coin counters, or do you have to stuff your pennies into those little paper tubes by yourself? (This is a matter of personal preference. Many betties enjoy the paper tubes, as long as they have a good fresh set of rubber gloves on hand.)
7. Are the lollipops securely wrapped in cellophane? Do they offer them to adults with no questions asked? (How nice!)

Betties are suspicious of the credit system. They prefer American Express to MasterCard.

Good betties become squeamish when they hear words like *mortgage, amortize,* and *arbitrage.* They are far more comfortable with the terms *compound interest* and *paid in full.*

Most betties believe that they are making an investment when they deposit a check in their savings account.

They steer clear of any markets that don't sell food.

They think stocks and bonds sound like instruments of torture rather than finance.

Betty children put pennies in their piggy banks from the time they are very young. When they are learning to count their toes, they always get sidetracked by wanting to know what this little piggy bought when he went to market. They never break their piggy banks with a hammer. Instead, when they take their puppies for a checkup, they bring their piggy banks along to the vet and ask him to operate.

You'll never catch the young betty putting a penny on the railroad tracks to watch it get squished.

Betties pay their bills the day they arrive. They never cheat or steal. They have no idea who Louis Rukeyser is. They love to go on shopping sprees, but they are never reckless about it. The good betty thinks that the way a person handles her money is a reflection of the state of her soul. She always requests new bills when she withdraws cash from the bank. Tipping people for services rendered embarrasses the betty. But she does it. She carries a calculator with her to make sure she always leaves the correct amount.

Betties love the accessories designed to carry money around. If they have to get physically close to literally filthy lucre, it eases the pain if the money comes out of a change purse, a good wallet, a shiny pocketbook, or a money belt.

Betties are frequently generous people. In one of those little contradictions that make the human race so fascinating, they can often be seen giving their money to beggars. This breaks all their rules of hygiene, but it reflects the deeper cleanliness of their spirits.

Betties can't understand it when they read headlines about people who have laundered their money. They do it all the time.

Just Buy It

Betties and advertising go together like locomotives and their clean steam engines: Advertising makes betties run . . . to the nearest shopping emporium, where they can stock up on their favorite products. If it weren't for advertising, how would the betty get the good news about what's out there? Other types might channel-surf during commercials, but the betty watches attentively, grocery list at hand. Aside from finding advertising helpful, betties love seeing *their* lifestyle depicted on the small screen. All those bright, clean, well-stocked kitchens! Advertisers sell the dream that betties actually live. They don't understand it when they read criticisms of the advertising industry that complain that real people don't live that way. *We* do, they think, and we're real. What could be more real than a gleaming white floor, a stain-resistant carpet, or a touching three-way telephone call? What more does anyone need?

The following are a few of betties' all-time favorite advertising campaigns.

The Breck Girl—models have included Brooke Shields and Jaclyn Smith.

Smith Barney—betties approve of them making money the old-fashioned way... by earning it.

Wheaties, "Breakfast of Champions"—especially when pint-sized betty Mary Lou Retton was featured on the box.

Ivory Soap, "so pure it floats"—who can argue with that?

Cotton, "the fabric of our lives"—betties love the clever use of the word fabric; for once, they get a double meaning.

The Doublemint twins—speaking of doubles! Betties love twins.

AT&T, "reach out and touch someone"—are you misting up just thinking about these heartrending mini-movies?

Bounty, "the quicker picker-upper"—er, why not?

Quaker Oats featuring Wilfred Brimley telling us, "It's the right thing to do"—Betties already know that, but it's nice to hear it on TV.

Nike, "just do it"—Yes!

Ikea, "it's a big country, someone's got to furnish it"—indeed.

Burger King, "have it your way"—one of the few situations in which this maxim applies to betties. And how about that great line "hold the pickles, hold the lettuce, special orders don't upset us." Way to go!

Betty Crocker. Betty was chosen in 1921 for its warm, friendly sound; Crocker was the last name for an emeritus director of the company. The portrait of Betty Crocker has been updated periodically since then, but she's never lost her essential bettiness. We'd know and love her anywhere!

Cyberbetties

Betties love their computers as dearly as they love their Cuisinarts. They employ them for a range of uses, from keeping track of every last red cent to typing up memos and reports to zipping off e-mail to other betties to "surfing" the Internet to entering the complete contents of their address books to generating zippy Christmas letters—well, you get the idea. While no up-to-the-minute betty worthy of the designation has a desk without a desktop and/or a lap without a laptop, the betty love of computers is a fairly recent development. Though by no means Luddites (how could any reasonable person be antitextile?), betties are, admittedly, slow to adapt to new technologies. One might even characterize them (technologically speaking only) as Johnny-come-latelies. As a result of such early misgivings, examples of betty misconceptions relating to computers abound:

TERM	MISCONCEPTION
UNIVAC	the ultimate vacuum cleaner
bits and bytes	something to serve with drinks or tea
hard drive	to the airport at rush hour
floppy disk	a warped LP record
MS-DOS	a proactive feminist leader (read: "Ms. Dos")
spreadsheet	something to picnic upon
cyberspace	a region explored by the *Starship Enterprise*

Now, however, most betties find that, at home or on the job, the personal computer is yet another labor-saving device they simply cannot do without. Never ones to avoid jumping on any passing bandwagon, the majority of betties are now fully aboard and ergonomically seated. They love to pepper their conversations with jargon that once seemed incomprehensible to them and pride themselves on how much RAM they have, the amount of megahertz their CPUs operate under, and the number of bps at which their modems can send and receive data. And with the slightest prodding, a betty computer enthusiast will gladly share helpful tips and advice on what to buy, where to buy it, and how to use it. As in all other areas of consumption, conspicuous and

otherwise, betties are highly prone to marketing, which may explain some of their computer favorites:

computer	Macintosh. (Also the betty's favorite raincoat.)
innovation	The mouse. (Despite a natural aversion to both "pointing" and "clicking.")
word-processing program	WordPerfect. (The name says it all.)
spreadsheet	Excel. (As all betties strive to do.)
icon	The little trash can. (Even more convenient and sanitary than the real thing.)
operation	Emptying the trash. (Betties can be overzealous in this direction and have been known to throw out files they actually need.)
application	Quicken. (The hands-down favorite. WARNING: Some betties have been known to become quite obsessive—entering every expenditure, spinning out numerous pie and bar charts, computing their net worth every day, and updating their portfolios with each market fluctuation.)

No matter how computer-literate betties may be, there is one line that they never cross: Betties are never hackers and, inversely, hackers are never betties. The very word *hacker* is unattractive, and the image it conjures of long greasy hair, cold-pizza breakfasts, and supercaffeinated cola drinks is enough to put a betty off her own light salad lunch. Why hack when you can be chatting? Computer betties have a language all their own. Study the following list to learn cyber shorthand:

BETTY CYBERCHAT SYMBOLS AND ABBREVIATIONS

(nota betty: turn page 90° to the right to see visual representation)

{}	a hug
*	a kiss
:)	a smile
:D	a big smile
:(	a frown
;)	a wink
:/	chagrin
:|	a bemused expression[†]
;|	hold on, my contact lens is bothering me[†]
@]––]––	a rose
@]–>–>––	a thorned rose
@]–––––––––	a dethorned, long-stemmed rose[†]
LO	laughing out loud
LAO	laughing ass off
LCC	Laughing Cow Cheese[†]
ROFLAO	rolling on floor laughing ass off
GGY	get a grip on yourself[†]
IMHO	in my humble opinion
TTY	talk to you
YBB!	you big betty![†]
BIABD	betty is as betty does[†]
<G>	grin
<EG>	evil grin
<VBG>	very big grin

[†]Of betty coinage.

Talk About It

Conversation is but carving!

Give no more to every guest

Than he's able to digest.

Give him always of the prime,

And but little at a time.

Carve to all but just enough,

Let them neither starve nor stuff,

And that you may have your due,

Let your neighbor starve for you.

—JONATHAN SWIFT

Here's a transcript of an actual conversation in a betty chat room. Why not "carve" one of your own today?

BKleen: salutation

Fondafax: hi, BKleen

IMNeat: greetings {}

TexBet: howdy, y'all :D

Fondafax: GGY, Tex

TexBet: sorry bout that :(

Fondafax: o.k. :|

LadyMcB: anyone know how to get out a spot? :/

BKleen: what kinda spot?

LadyMcB: a darned spot

TexBet: <G> spot remover

IMNeat: club soda works well

Fondafax: did TexBet say g-spot remover?

BKleen: can you be more explicit, Lady?

TexBet: that was a grin, Fonda

IMNeat: or baking soda and water

Fondafax: just joshing, Tex :)

LadyMcB: :/blood

IMNeat: a sloution of one teaspoon white vinegar to one gallon of water works

   well on floors

BKleen: what kind of blood?

TexBet: <VBG> blood remover!

IMNeat: diluted vinegar also works well on glass surfaces

Fondafax: LCC, Tex

LadyMcB: u know, blood blood

TexBet: TTY in private, Fonda? @]————————

BKleen: ;| blood blood? You didn't kill anyone did you, Lady?

IMNeat: the problem with vinegar, of course, is the smell <sigh>

Fondafax: in your dreams, Tex

LadyMcB: YBB! BKleen LO

IMNeat: did i type sloution? sorry bout the typo, Betties

LadyMcB: didn't want to mention it, IM, but BIABD

BKleen: seriously, Lady, what kind of blood?

IMNeat: bloods a tuff one

TexBet: c'mon, Fonda * * {}{} i'm rich and hung like a horse <EG>

ADMINISTRATOR: Bye, Tex

Fondafax: phew! who let him in? besides, i'm a straight guy, not that there's

anything wrong with other kinds of preferences

IMNeat: consulting my stain guide

BKleen: kitchen timer went off, gotta go. bye

Fondafax: bye, B

LadyMcB: someone's at the door, ciao

Fondafax: Avon calling?

IMNeat: hmmm. cold water and salt might do the trick

Fondafax: c u, LadyMcB. my dryer's buzzing, gotta get my shirts out before
they wrinkle

IMNeat: or you could consult an expert i know a good dry cleaner in Blatimore
did wonders with grape juice on a lace tablecloth

IMNeat: did i just type Blatimore :|?

IMNeat: i'm glad i don't have any bloodstains apple juice is tough, too. the
pectin

IMNeat: the worst stain i ever had was mustard on a silk cravat

IMNeat: or maybe it was grass on the knees of my white jodhpurs

IMNeat: or perhaps . . .

We're going to break off here, but remember, other like-minded betties are only a keystroke away. So get out your Q-tips and your antistatic dust rag and find a new friend on your clean computer. And when you're reading your e-mail, you may want to allow yourself to get all warm and fuzzy inside by knowing that somewhere, at the exact same moment, that big betty Bill Gates is probably reading his, too.

Trains and Boats and Planes

Homebodies that they are, it's difficult for betties to travel.[17] Packing and unpacking are within their domain, but travel conditions and what's at the end of a journey are another, scarier matter. The big hotel chains understand these fears and have done what they can to assure the reluctant traveler that she will at least find comfortable and sanitary surroundings in the confines of her room. Howard Johnson, Marriott,[18] Hilton, Best Western, et bettera, have all done their share to make the world a smaller, cleaner, bettier place. Many betties take advantage of the weekend packages offered by the chains in order to have a getaway without getting away from the comforts of home. But, every so often, the betty spirit is stirred by the prospect of seeing unfamiliar sights and exploring the larger world. The following is a list of places that betties can visit that correspond with their sensitive sensibilities:

[17]For a comprehensive portrayal of a betty's trepidation with regard to far-flung places, please read Ann Tyler's novel *The Accidental Tourist*.
[18]Betty businessmen love Courtyard by Marriott.

Top Ten Betty Destinations

10. Canada
Mounties, clean water, Toronto.

9. Club Med for Families
Fun for the whole group, beads instead of money, adorable kiddie song-and-dance shows at the end of the week.

8. Japan
Home of the biggest betties on earth. Come for the tea ceremony, stay for the bathhouses.

7. Germany
You don't know what table manners are until you see how these folks instruct their children.

6. The Benelux Countries
Heavenly (as opposed to sinful) chocolates, tulips, tulips, tulips, scenic canals.

5. San Francisco
Cable cars, that big betty bridge, Ghirardelli Square, Alcatraz *in the distance,* the bay.

4. Washington, D.C.
The White House, the Smithsonian costume exhibit, the Mall.

3. Vatican City
The newly cleaned Sistine Chapel, chasubles galore, the pope.

2. Disney World and Epcot Center
A completely manufactured betty environment. This is as close as any betty should ever get to Morocco.

1. Switzerland
Everything on time, fondue, chalets, yodeling, home of the International Red Cross!

So bon voyage, Betty! And remember,

- roll your clothes so they won't wrinkle

- take a few Polaroids of the contents of your suitcase for insurance purposes[19]

- don't carry packages across borders for anyone, no matter how cute he is[20]

- bring along a travel iron and a clothes steamer

- don't drink the water ANYWHERE

- have fun!

---

[19]Sometimes empathetic customs inspectors can be persuaded to accept these in lieu of actually rifling through your things. Sometimes not.

[20]Sad but true—because of their polite, helpful natures, betties can be duped into *trafficking drugs*.

Keep America Bettiful!

I, Elizabeth "Betty" Albright, can't vouch for the BQ of the following towns, but at least they sound promising. Doesn't it warm the cockles of your heart to see how chock-full o' bettiness America is?

Alabama
Citronelle
Normal
Reform

Arizona
Florence
Goodyear
Snowflake

Arkansas
Cotton Plant
Sweet Home

California
Blythe
Gerber
Happy Camp
Nice

Colorado
Brush
Fairplay
Sugar City

Connecticut
Ivoryton

Delaware
Bridgeville

Florida
Bowling Green
Cocoa
Frostproof
Sink Creek
Sunniland

Georgia
Commerce
Lumber City
Social Circle

Idaho
Challis
Gooding
Soda Springs

Illinois
Bureau
Equality
Sparta

Indiana
Lapel
Paragon
Spiceland

Iowa
Bettendorf
Early
What Cheer

Kansas

Labette
Pretty Prairie
Protection

Kentucky

Betsy Lane
Combs
Longview
Sassafras

Louisiana

Waterproof
Welcome

Maine

Friendship
Unity
Woolwich

Maryland

Seat Pleasant
Shell Town

Massachusetts

Sandwich
Tea Ticket

Michigan

Mackinaw City
Parchment
Schoolcraft

Minnesota

Comfrey
Le Center
Proctor
Young America

Mississippi

Ecru
Kiln
Ruleville
Tie Plant

Missouri

Bland
Butler
Hale

Montana

Belfry
Brady
Three Forks

Nebraska

Alliance
Friend
Osmond

Nevada

Blue Diamond
Zephyr Cove

New Hampshire

Bow Guild

New Jersey

Egg Harbor City
Fellowship
Scotch Plains

New Mexico

Mountainair
Reserve
Truth or Conse-
quences

New York

Lake Success
Painted Post
Vestal

North Carolina

Bonnie Doone
Cashiers
Mint Hill
Toast

North Dakota
Cando
Kindred
Plaza

Ohio
Excello
Gratis
Mentor

Oklahoma
Dill City
McCurtain
Sterling

Oregon
Drain
Riddle
Sisters

Pennsylvania
Confluence
Fairchange
Library
Snowshoe

Rhode Island
Common Fence
  Point

South Carolina
Couchtown
Travelers Rest

South Dakota
Box Elder
Tea

Tennessee
Bakewell
Mascot
Wrigley

Texas
Blanket
Cloverleaf
Comfort
Groom
Happy

Utah
Bountiful
Enterprise
Plain City

Vermont
Darby

Virginia
Banner
Rural Retreat
Wise

Washington
Country Homes
Electric City
Soap
Lake

West Virginia
Big Chimney
Clothier
Reader

Wisconsin
Argyle
Combined Locks
Land O'Lakes

Wyoming
Bar Nunn
Basin
Reliance

A Dull Betty

Betties subscribe to the concept of a golden mean and know that the happiest lives are balanced lives. So while attending to one's betiquette and bettying around the office are important and fulfilling activities, betties also need another dimension to their existence to make their lives complete. Creation is all well and good, but recreation has its place, too. Even God rested on the seventh day. So now, let's take a look at what betties do when they want to sit back, relax, and let their hair down.[21]

[21]This is okay, as long as the hair is clean and well groomed.

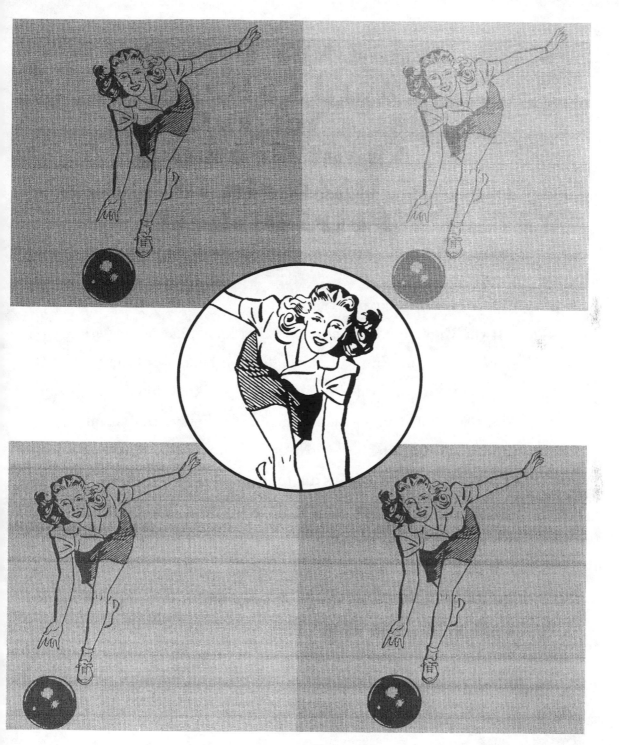

the betty at play

When She Uses the Word *Culture*, She's Not Talking About Growing Bacteria in Petri Dishes!

What do betties do to have fun?

If you've been paying attention, you know that betties are capable of having fun in nearly any situation because of their enlightened bettitude toward life. But they also like to have special fun. Fun for its own sake. Fun, fun, fun 'til their parental units take their motor vehicles away. (Not really, of course; they'd never go that far, but sometimes it's fun to pretend to be naughty . . . and to imagine what Daddy's going to do to his disobedient little girl. . . . Uh-oh, let's not go there!)

Which brings us back to our original question: What do betties do to have fun? Let us name the ways! But first, to lighten up the mood, here's a betty riddle. . . .

What do betties name their dogs?

SPOTLESS!

Betties Read

Books. Magazines. Labels. Cereal boxes. And, above all, the fine print. The following are a few of the characteristic behaviors of reading betties. They are the people who…

- visit libraries with the same anticipation that the cast of the Howard Stern show visits strip clubs

- make note of words they don't know and look them up in the dictionary

- use bookmarks

- never write in their books, unless they are very famous betties whose marginalia might add to the font of human knowledge

- dust their dust jackets

- make wish lists of items they want from *Levenger's Catalog for Serious Readers*

- take it personally when they hear someone crack the spine of a new book

- read literary biographies

- take being called bookish as a compliment

- think bifocals look stylish

- blissfully smell the pages of freshly printed books

- read for *fun*

No one is happier than the betty to discover a book that is deep, beautiful, and expressive of the highest human values. But, unfortunately, the betty's respect for appearance often serves her wrong when it comes to literature. When browsing in the bookstore, the betty is liable to be moved to make a purchase on the basis of a title, only to be disappointed later by the contents. Yet in spite of occasional unpleasant surprises, the betty still, more often than not, judges a book by its cover.

Top Ten Betty Book Titles

1. *The Just So Stories*, by Rudyard Kipling

2. *Housekeeping*, by Marilyn Robinson

3. *Starting from Scratch*, by Rita Mae Brown

4. *Betty*, by George Simenon

5. *The Seven Habits of Highly Effective People*, by Steven R. Covey

6. *Raise High the Roofbeam, Carpenters*, by J. D. Salinger

7. *Chicken Soup for the Soul*, by Jack Canfield and Mark Victor

   Hansen

8. *The Rule of Saint Benedict*[22]

9. *The Bell Jar*, by Sylvia Plath

10. *Stop the Insanity!*, by Susan Powter

Once they do get past the superficialities, betties tend to be careful and attentive readers. The following is a list of books that have met their standards, again and again:

[22]Or *The Way of Perfection*, by Saint Teresa of Avila.

All-Time Favorites

Little Women, by Louisa May Alcott

Little House on the Prairie, by Laura Ingalls Wilder

Life's Little Instruction Book,[23] by H. Jackson Brown Jr.

A Tree Grows in Brooklyn, by Betty Smith

A Child's Garden of Verses, by Robert Louis Stevenson

The Road Less Traveled, by M. Scott Peck

The Nun's Story,[24] by Kathryn Hulme

Leaves of Grass, by Walt Whitman

Cross Creek, by Marjorie Kinnan Rawlings

The Story of a Soul, by Saint Thérèse of Lisieux

The Good Earth, by Pearl S. Buck

Gifts from the Sea, by Anne Morrow Lindbergh

---

[23] "Little" in the title is a good sign.
[24] Similarly, *In This House of Brede,* by Rumer Godden.

The Alphabetty

Here's a primer that will teach your children the alphabet and provide them with friendly examples of betty behavior at the same time.

A is for Alice who waxed the floor

B is for Betty who waxed it some more

C is for Carol who tidied her room

D is for Derek who's quick with a broom

E is for Edith who scoured the tub

F is for Franny who gave the candlesticks a rub

G is for Gertrude who made a great fuss, when

H, sister Harriet, forgot the Glass Plus

I is for Irma who mulched her garden

J is for Jerome, who asks everyone's pardon

K is for Ken who enlisted in the navy

L is for Len who thrice strains his gravy

M is for Mona whose last name is Lisa

N is for Nino who always blots his pizza

O is for Oscar who buffs up his shoes

P is for Prissie who wears gloves to read the news

Q is for Quentin who wears bow ties with flair

R is for Rupert who conditions his hair

S is for Simon who says what to do

T is for Tommy who replies, fudge you!

U is for Ursula who designs window treatments

V is for Vera who shares her Junior Mints

W is for Winifred who loves to sew and mend

X is for Ex-Lax, a betty's good friend

Y is for Yolanda who creates Yuletide logs

Z is for Zelda who listens to Mozart while she jogs

Extra, Extra, Read All About It!

Although they fear newsprint,[25] betties love newspapers, especially human interest stories, the crime blotter, the home and living sections, reviews, letters to the editor, the advertisements, and editorials. In other words, they like pretty much everything except for the news. Certain headlines are liable to attract their attention, however. The following are examples of headlines that have coaxed betties to read on:

Scientists Discover Surefire Cure for
Ring-Around-the-Collar

India's First Annual National Clean-up Day

Man Wins Betty Crocker Bake-Off

Pillsbury Dough Boy Becomes Las Vegas
Lounge Lizard
Burnt out at a tender age

Charles Manson Cleans Up His Act
"No more Helter-Skelter for me," says Charlie

Seinfeld's Kitchen Cabinets Win Design Award

Geraldo Rivera Unearths the Medicine
Cabinet of Dr. Caligari

An Apple a Day Linked to Rapid Weight Loss

[25]The biggest betties have special gloves that they wear to read the paper. Others carry towelettes or read in a location where they have access to soap and water.

Betties Watch Movies and Television

Who do you think invented built-in drink holders on movie theater seats, and TV dinners? When they're finished with their chores for the day, betties love to get comfortable on the sofa or in the Barcalounger and watch their favorite shows. Even in the nineties, a trip to the  movie theater is considered big-time fun by the life-loving betty. They don't understand why anyone would hate a town (Hollywood) or an appliance (the television set). They are staunch supporters of the First Amendment and leave it up to individuals to police their own intake. Remember, everything in moderation!

Here are some of the top betty picks in the realm of filmed entertainment.

The Big Betty Film Festival

Featuring Some of the
Favorite Betty Films Ever

Walk in a sourpuss, walk out a believer. And there'll be crocks of fresh popcorn and boxes of jujubes for all!

1.
The Sound of Music

The musical genre is betty, as are nearly all musicals, but this is the Grand Kahuna of them all, a betty masterpiece. Raindrops on roses, whiskers on kittens, play clothes made from sturdy drapes, Austria, the gazebo, nuns, the puppet show, and the betty, spit-and-polish side of the Nazi occupation. Betty wonders how many times Princess Diana saw this one when she was growing up. That haircut—just a coincidence? Betties, even princesses, all want to be Maria.

2.
The Trouble with Angels

There's a glitch with the racy band uniforms, but Hayley Mills becomes a nun at the end. Calling all Good Girls.

3.
It's a Wonderful Life

This film fulfills a secret betty fantasy that everyone would really miss us were we gone. Live, Jimmy Stewart, live! We root for you year after year.

4.
Bye Bye Birdie (both versions)

Chynna Phillips is a bigger betty than Ann-Margret, but Dick Van Dyke rules 4 ever.

5.
Serial Mom

Beverly (Kathleen Turner) kills a woman for not rewinding a videotape! John Waters knows from bettiness.

6.
Funny Face

Audrey Hepburn as a bookstore clerk turned model. Think pink, Betty!

7.
Your personal pick of a Shirley Temple flick

8.
Help!

The Fabs do cute in scenic locales.

9.
Mommie Dearest

Not for the weak of stomach but a good solid betty cautionary tale that makes a point about the undesirability of wire hangers and gives a good demonstration of how not to prune your rose garden.

10.
Clueless

Based on Jane Austen; cute outfits; and Alicia Silverstone uses the word *betty*.

Isn't Hollywood great?
Not always. . . .

The First Annual Devil's Triangle Film Festival

Let's hope this festival disappears and takes these films with it forever!

1.
The Texas Chainsaw Massacre

Barbecue, anyone?

2.
Pink Flamingos

Pup poop, anyone?

3.
Easy Rider

Easy for Dennis Hopper!

4.
Koyaanisqatsi

Philip Glass orchestrates demolition. Ouch!

5.
Eraserhead

Antichild, antifamily, anti—steam heat. David Lynch acts out big time.

6.
Los Olvidados

Luis Buñuel's depiction of poor children. Gross beyond belief.

7.
Porky's/Animal House

Boys will be "pigs."

8.
120 Days of Sodom

The title says it.

9.
The Rocky Horror Picture Show

Don't dream it, be it? Very dangerous stuff!

10.
Mondo Cane and Mondo Cane 2

Try to make an argument for man's being innately good after seeing this. *Oi vay.*

The Betty Zone

Luckily, as television has to answer to its advertisers, it rarely falls as far as films have. But here's a listing of imaginary Sunday evening television programming that would set any betty's dentures on edge.

	7:00	7:30	8:00
3 WMOP	**Lifestyles of the Rich and Famous** Caviar nightmares disrupt Morgan Fairchild's trip to The Hague.	**Family Affair** Buffy and Jody find Nazi paraphernalia in Mr. French's drawers.	**The Brady Bunch** Cindy sees Peter in the shower.
4 WDAB	**Bewitched** Endora turns Darrin into a gypsy.	**The Flying Nun** An ill wind diverts Sister Bertrille to Iraq.	**Charlie's Angels** A sag in the ratings forces the Angels to don brassieres. Guest star: Jane Russell
6 WCUP	**The Betty White Show** Betty is unfriendly to a neighbor.	**The Donna Reed Show** Mary (Shelley Fabares) dates a drummer. Guest Star: Keith Moon.	**The Doris Day Show** Thinking she's dreaming, Doris shows up for work in the nude.
8 WTEA	**The Patty Duke Show** A hot dog makes Cathy lose control.	**The Courtship of Eddie's Father** Eddie learns that Mrs. Livingston is his biological mother.	**Little House on the Prairie** Charles reneges on his FHA mortgage and is sent to the Big House.
13 WEGG	**The French Chef** Fun with tripe.	**This Old House** Chemical remedies for insect infestations.	**Nova** "The Center Does Not Hold." An inquiry into entropy.

8:30	9:00	10:00
That Girl Ann Marie lands a part in *Hair*.	**The Love Boat** Panic holds the crew in its deadly grip when the *Pacific Princess* is rammed by an oil tanker. Guest stars: Sean Penn, Courtney Love.	**Las Vegas 75th Anniversary Special** Host: Hunter S. Thompson.
	Movie of the Week: "Whatchamacallit?" Starring Martha Plimpton, Lisa Bonet, Drew Barrymore. Coeds tease roommate (Melissa Gilbert) suddenly afflicted with dysphasia.	
The Mary Tyler Moore Show Rhoda binges; Mary purges.	**The Waltons** Thinking Christmas has become too commercial, the family makes a pact never to celebrate it again.	**ER** A visiting proctologist rides Dr. Ross for making a misdiagnosis
	T.V. Movie: "Out, Out, Darn Spot!" Barry Bostwick stars as a sea captain whose marriage and career run aground when he can't stop washing his hands.	
Frontline A day at the abattoir.	**American Playhouse: Bret Easton Ellis's "American Psycho"** Starring Mickey Rourke.	

You Can Fool Some of the People Some of the Time, but Never a Betty . . .

Have you ever heard tell of actors complaining about certain lines in their scripts on the basis of a gut feeling that "my character wouldn't say that"? Please think twice before you decide they're being obnoxious; there's a chance they're right. But when it comes to their characters' essential bettiness, they needn't worry, for in spite of the shifting plot lines that often turn a good character bad and vice versa, it's usually possible to get a betty read on a television character that really doesn't change no matter what he or she does. Likewise, basically rotten types might occasionally do good deeds—on television, this passes for complexity—but they don't really fool the betty, now do they?

But let's not belabor the point philosophically. Experience is the best teacher, *n'est-ce pas?* Below are lists of some of the characters from several top TV shows. You decide whether or not they are basically betties. Put a check in the column next to their names. Don't think too hard. This is knowledge you intuitively have in your heart.

	Essentially Betty	At Heart, NOT!
Seinfeld		
Jerry		
George		
Kramer		
Elaine		

	Essentially Betty	At Heart, NOT!
Melrose Place		
Kimberley		
Jane		
Billy		
Alison		
Sidney		
Michael		
Peter		
Jake		
Jo		
Matt		

Friends	**Essentially Betty**	**At Heart, NOT!**
Rachel		
Monica		
Joey		
Chandler		
Ross		
Phoebe		

Beverly Hills 90210	**Essentially Betty**	**At Heart, NOT!**
Brenda		
Donna		
Steve		
Brandon		
Kelly		
Valerie		
Dylan		

Dateline	**Essentially Betty**	**At Heart, NOT!**
Jane Pauley		
Stone Phillips		

20/20	**Essentially Betty**	**At Heart, NOT!**
Barbara Walters		
Hugh Downs		

Beavis & Butt-head	**Essentially Betty**	**At Heart, NOT!**
Beavis		
Butt-head		

Now for the correct answers . . .

Guess what? Whatever *you* decided is correct! By now you know enough to make these judgments yourself. I didn't want to tell you ahead of time that you weren't actually going to be graded, knowing how nervous this might make you feel. But, hey! Here you are, in command of a brand-new skill! Doesn't it feel great? And you can apply these labels to any character on any show. Or try it in the airport as you people-watch! But remember—not all police are betties at heart, in spite of the spiffy uniforms. It's wisest to keep your opinions to yourself. . . .

The betty
AT PLAY

145

Bettywood

Autobiographical details aside, these folks come across as betties time after time.

Hall of Fame

Doris Day

Sandra Dee

Gene Kelly

Shirley Temple

Annette Funicello

Margaret Dumont

Fred Astaire

Julie Andrews

Grace Kelly

Barbara Bel Geddes

Busby Berkeley

Glenn Ford

Spring Byington

Bing Crosby

Don Defore

Gary Cooper

Henry Fonda

Shirley Jones

Deborah Kerr

James MacArthur

Ralph Macchio

Adolphe Menjou

Dina Merrill

Hayley Mills

Pat Morita

Ronald Reagan

Katharine Ross

Esther Williams

Frank Capra

Preston Sturges

Billy Wilder

Roy Rogers

Dale Evans

Trigger

Betty Television Stars

Carol Burnett

Mary Tyler Moore

Alan Alda

Captain Kangaroo

Scott Baio

Ted Bessell

Karen Valentine

Shirley Booth

Kirk Cameron

Candace Cameron

Richard Thomas

Tom Selleck

Macdonald Carey

Susan St. James

Donna Reed

Linda Purl

Jay North

Gary Coleman

Gary Collins

Juliet Mills

Lee Meriwether

Kellie Martin

Will Smith

Dennis Day

Patty Duke Astin

Lea Thompson

Meredith Baxter

Kristy McNichol

Shelley Long

Jane Seymour

Melissa Gilbert

Dwayne Hickman

Tracy Gold

Tracy Nelson

Courteney Cox

Gale Gordon

Elizabeth Montgomery

Betty White

Patrick Duffy

Jerry Seinfeld

Paul Reiser

The betty AT PLAY

Current Betty Oscar Contenders

Kevin Costner

Tom Cruise

Denzel Washington

Robert Redford

Meg Ryan

Michael J. Fox

Harrison Ford

Emma Thompson

Matthew Broderick

Ellen Burstyn

Phoebe Cates

Sally Field

Tom Hanks

Ron Howard

Bright Brites, Big Betty

A Betty Novelette

You're not the kind of girl who would *ordinarily* lie in bed until *nine in the morning,* but because it is *your thirtieth birthday,* you've decided *it can't hurt* to sleep late, *just this once.* Yet when your eyes open, you find that it is seven *o'clock as usual.* You're such *a creature of habit. Oh, well,* it's *nice* to have a couple of extra hours on your hands. If anyone knows how to put free *time* to *good use,* it's you!

You stretch your arms over your head and *appreciate* how *rested* you feel. *Thank goodness* for your *Sealy Posturepedic.* Everyone teased you about *saving up* for it, but you *know in your heart* that you made *the right choice.* If you'd spent that money on *a weekend visit* to New York,[26] as *your friends suggested,* what would you have to show for it now? Nothing but *a pair* of picked *pockets,* probably.[27] You prefer to *invest* in *items* of *lasting value.* The mattress *should* last for a full *decade,* at least, and, because you'll be *sleeping well,* you'll have the energy to make *enough money* to *save* for another. There's nothing like *long-term planning* to make life *meaningful.* You *credit* it with staving off those painful bouts of existential anxiety that plague your less *focused friends.* The *prospect* of seeing *your plans come to fruition* is as good as any[28] a *reason* to live. If only everyone would develop *clear, achievable goals, the world*[29] would be *a happier place. Certainly* everyone you know could *pull themselves together* enough *to save for a mattress.* Sometimes it makes you a *tad* bit[30] impatient that they choose to spend their money on frivolities instead, but *you know better* than *to offer* your opinion[31] when it hasn't been sought. You'd hate to become *a busybody* this early in your life. That's *an occupation* for *old ladies, God bless them.*

---

[26]New York is not a betty destination, although that might change after the Disney Company performs its magic on Times Square.

[27]Mathematical probability is betty, but in everyday life the interjection of probability into a situation is a no-no.

[28]As good as any, suggests a bit too much leeway to qualify as a betty expression.

[29]The earth isn't particularly betty; the world is. Think of the difference between *house* and *home.*

[30]There are plethora of words like *bit,* and phrases in this novelette that, although they can be betty under the right circumstances, also have non-betty connotations. Henceforth, in these footnotes, these examples will be given the abbreviation NBC.

[31]Opinions are betty. No such claim can be made as to their content.

Before doing anything else, you always *make your bed*, and today is *no exception*. You form your *hospital corners* as well as any *orderly*. As you *plump up* your *European square pillows* with their *280-thread-count 100-percent cotton shams*, you think about all the *fun* you're going to have today, once you get over *feeling guilty* for being *at home* on *a work day* when you're not sick. *Honestly*, you wouldn't mind being at *your job* as the *accessories editor* for *a fashion magazine*, but your *company* has a *policy* of giving *employees* their *birthday* off, and you're not the *type* to buck the *system*. *Nevertheless*, you were *uneasy* about it until *your boyfriend reassured* you that it was really okay to take the day off. He's so *nice* and *cute* that if he *asked you to marry* him, you'd say yes, yes, yes![32] You know exactly who you'd ask to be your *bridesmaids*, and you'd definitely want a big *rehearsal dinner* with lots of champagne and funny *toasts*. You become nervous just thinking of how much planning it would take. You'd need a new *file box* full of *index cards* and *dividers* and probably a *three-ring binder* filled with *pre-reinforced paper*, too. Of course, you could keep some of your *lists and reminders* on your *laptop computer*, but somehow it seems more *appropriate* to do the *planning* for the only *wedding* you'll ever have in our own *neat handwriting*. Anyway, someone will probably give you an *official wedding planner*, with all the *categories* you need to consider already laid out[33] for you, so all you have to do is *fill in the blanks*. That way, you'll be sure not to skip[34] any important steps on the way to *the altar!* You *smile* as you think of how much you love *weddings*, largely because they *require* so much *stationery*.

The bed being made, you step into your *Dearfoams* and walk to *the window to see what* the weather is like today. You're in *luck! The sun is shining, the sky is clear, and the clouds are high and fluffy;* they're just the kind that look like animals or *funny characters* when you lie on your back[35] on a patch of *sweet-smelling grass* and look up at the sky using your *imagination.*[36] You *guesstimate the temperature* to be a balmy[37] seventy to *seventy-five degrees,*

[32]Yes, yes, yes. Remember the Meg Ryan fake orgasm scene in *When Harry Met Sally*? She gave this expression an NBC. At that moment, she was a BRA, that is, a Betty Run Amok.

[33]Laid, laid out—both have NBCs.

[34]In this context, the word *skip* has an NBC; but skipping stones or skipping down the sidewalk are, of course, very betty.

[35]Lie on your back—NBC.

[36]See "opinions," note 31.

[37]NBC.

cool enough for *a cotton sweater,* warm enough to *forgo* your *down vest.* Soon it will be *that time of year again* when you pack[38] your *seasonal* clothes in *Ziploc freezer bags* and *store* them at the back of your *closet* for the summer, which is *the best you can do* within the *confines* of your *apartment.* Wouldn't it be great to have a *cedar closet* for summer *storage* like your *maternal grandparents* do? *Oh, well,* maybe *someday!*

You go to *the bathroom.* This is a part of life you could skip altogether, but as it's not likely that anyone is going to *invent* a way to *dispense* with basic bodily *functions* in *your lifetime,* you've developed a *series of coping strategies* to get you through the un*pleasantness.* In essence, you followed the *advice* given to *squeamish Victorian ladies* to enable them to *tolerate* the base desires of their *husbands:* You close your eyes and think of *England.* Or you fix[39] your gaze on the *Crabtree and Evelyn matching soap dish* and *toothbrush cup* that you bought to *reward* yourself for *maintaining your ideal weight* for yet another year. So far, you haven't had the heart to use them; they're just too *pretty.* You keep your *soap* and *toothbrush* in the *shower instead.* You're very excited this *morning* because *your best friend* gave you an early *birthday present* of French[40] *washcloths (gants de bain)* and you're going to use them— one of them, that is—for *the very first time.* It is *sewn together* on three sides so it slips over your whole hand like *a loofah,* but unlike *a loofah,* it won't fall to pieces[41] in *the washing machine.* You step into the stall for your *first shower of the day,* turning on *your shower radio* as you adjust *the temperature.* The *washcloth* is both *adorable* and *practical!* You wonder why no one has thought of *manufacturing* them here. After all, if you like them, won't everybody?

"Three convicts escaped overnight from the local *peniteni*ary," says the radio. "*Police* are *combing* the surrounding *neighborhoods* and have warned the *citizenry* to keep all doors and windows *locked.* These men should be *considered* armed and dangerous."

How awful! you think. You quickly spin the dial to *a soft rock station* and try to put the news out of your mind,[42] yet you cannot help feeling that those men *shouldn't have done the crime if they couldn't do the time.* Grown-ups

[38]NBC, as in packing heat.
[39]NBC, as in "I need a . . ."
[40]See "New York," note 26. And Disney didn't make a difference there.
[41]"Fall to pieces"—a betty nightmare.
[42]"Out of your mind"—ditto.

have to take *responsibility* for their actions! Oh, well, I *suppose it takes all kinds,* you think as you take your *dental floss* from the *shower caddy.* It's one of your charming quirks[43] that you like *to floss* in *the shower.* This *mint-flavored floss* is such *a treat,* you *wish* they would *flavor* the *floss* with chocolate[44] and *butterscotch as well.* Now it's time *to wash* your hair. *Let's see,* which *shampoo* will it be today? *Neutrogena,* to remove the residue buildup, or *good* old *reliable Herbal Essences,* which *experts* say is better than many of the more expensive *shampoo formulas.* You allow the lather[45] to remain in your hair for three minutes, then you begin to *rinse thoroughly.* Uh-oh . . . Doesn't it sound like someone is walking around outside the *bathroom?* Someone with, perhaps, a *knife?* You remember what happened to *Janet Leigh* in *Psycho,* and you make every *effort* to hasten your *ablutions* along. You *wrap* yourself in your *extra-thirsty bathsheet* and *press* your ear to the door. All is *quiet*—of course. As you cream[46] your legs with *Jergen's Lotion,* you chide yourself for being *such a ninny.* Of course a psychotic *serial* murderer isn't after you! You're probably just a little jittery from the news of the escaped convicts in *your neighborhood.* You *remind* yourself that it's never *prudent* to feel too overly *secure,* so you decide you have no need to feel *embarrassed* for having a *mild case* of *the heebie-jeebies.*

Back in your room, you pick out your *clothes* for the day, starting with your underwear and your *kneesocks.* You have tried many different brands,[47] but nobody makes then quite like *Bonnie Doone!* Today you choose a *camel color,* which will go well with any one of the many *tartan plaid scarves* that you have been *collecting* since you were a teenager.[48] Like *Prince Charles,* you *love* anything *Scottish!* You open your *closet*—you still feel *a little bit frustrated* that other people started *closet-organizing businesses* before you could get up the nerve to do it yourself, because you had the idea[49] *ages ago*—and *peruse your wardrobe.* It makes you *happy* just to see everything hanging[50] there, all *ironed* and *dry-cleaned* and fragrant. You could stand here for a long time,

[43]Betties are suspicious of charm and quirks. What's wrong with being direct?
[44]Too tempting and addictive to be betty.
[45]NBC.
[46]NBC.
[47]Ask the cows how they feel about this word.
[48]See "opinions," note 31.
[49]Ditto.
[50]NBC.

just looking, if you allowed yourself that kind of leisure.[51] But *time's a wasting,* so you make your choices. Today you take out one of your old *Liberty paisley-print shirtwaist dresses,* and a 100 percent wool sweater with a *grosgrain ribbon* on the *button placket.* You slip into your favorite *navy blue Belgian shoes,* and top[52] it all off with a *tortoiseshell headband,* a *pair* of *pearl earrings,* and *a light dusting of powder* across your cheeks. You glance in the *mirror*—you try to keep your *mirror time* to a minimum, there's something *unseemly* about staring at *oneself* for too long—and are pleased with your trim,[53] *neat appearance.* If anyone happens to drop by now with an early *birthday treat* for you, you're *ready* to *greet* them.

Readiness is all!

You head to the *kitchen* for *breakfast.* You make no bones about the *fact* that the *kitchen* is your *favorite* room in the house. Seeing all of your *appliances* arrayed across the *counters positively makes your day.*[54] Having set the *timer* on your *coffee maker* the night before, your coffee is just *ready* to pour as you slip your *oat bran toaster waffle* into your *widemouthed toaster.* You take a *gaily striped* cloth *napkin* and *utensils* from the *kitchen* drawers and set a *cheerful* place at the *little* table you had *custom made* for your *breakfast nook.* When your *breakfast* is ready, you turn on[55] the *television* to see if there are any big *stars* on *the morning talk shows.* (This is *a treat, just for today.*[56] *Usually* you don't *read* or watch anything while you eat, having heard that it's better for your *digestion* not to.) *Oh, wow! Joan Lunden* is *interviewing Ron Howard.* You've always liked *his work,* ever since he played *Opie* on *The Andy Griffith Show.* As you slip on your *rubber gloves* to *wash the dishes* (you prefer the *Rubbermaid* brand to *Playtex,* because you just aren't *comfortable* with the idea of Living Gloves), you think about how much you loved *Apollo 13* and *wonder* when some *bright* young *studio executive* is going to think of making *a prequel.* Even as *a made-for-TV movie,* it would be *welcome.* And what *a casting coup* it would be if they could get *Tom Hanks* again. But as he wasn't even *nominated* for an Oscar[57] for his *role* as the brave *astronaut Jim*

---

[51]This is borderline. So much to do with leisure—the suit, for example—is betty, but the image of all that free time is a bit scarifying.

[52]NBC, viz S&M.

[53]NBC. Enough said.

[54]Betty, in spite of Clint Eastwood's ironic line reading.

[55]NBC.

[56]One of the slogans of Betties Anonymous and other twelve-steppers.

[57]Emmy is betty; Oscar is not. Grammy is bettiest of all!

Lovell, he might not be *interested.* Then again, you tell yourself, maybe *acclaim* means nothing to him. You don't really have any idea what he thinks, do you now? *It's not fair* to make assumptions,[58] is it? Of course, it would be difficult for *Tom Hanks* to play a younger *version* of himself, even with the best of *Hollywood's makeup magic.* He'd probably have to *play Mr. Lovell, Jim's dad,* or perhaps a *president.* You feel *pity* for him for *a moment,* thinking of how his range[59] of *roles* will diminish now that he's getting older. But, hey, you're not getting any younger yourself, *sister!* Don't forget, you are thirty thirty thirty thirty. . . . It's enough to give anyone a headache. You take *two Excedrin* and swallow them with the *help of grapefruit juice,* which you've *read* is *supposed to* make *medicines* more *effective.* Sounds like *a thrifty tip* to you!

You turn off the *TV* and decide to *listen* to a *CD* instead. Let's see, now, will it be *The Beatles* or *Paul McCartney*[60] in his *solo* incarnation? You look through your *alphabetized collection. Music* is so nice. Lately you've really been *enjoying The Smiths,* whose *CD's* you bought on the basis of the *name* of the band. *Luckily the lead singer* has a really *melodious* voice, even if you don't know *exactly* what he's talking about. In the end you turn to your old *record collection* and *decide* to *listen* to *George Harrison's All Things Must Pass,* which *sets just the right mood* for *your birthday* by *reminding* you that *on the one hand,* the fact that you are getting older is meaningless in the larger scheme of things,[61] but *on the other hand,* in the here and now, it *sure* feels important to *you!*

Time to go to your *desk* and *write* a few *letters.* If *letter writing truly* becomes a lost art, as the cultural *Gloomy Gusses* are always predicting,[62] it's not going to be *your fault!* As you pick up[63] your *Montblanc ballpoint pen,* you think back *fondly* to when *your parents* gave it to you just after you gave *the valedictory speech* at your *graduation* from *dental school. Gosh,* was that *a Kodak moment!* You take out your *engraved Crane's notepaper*—actually, you've succumbed to *thermography* for your more casual *writing paper, in order to*

[58] The fair-minded betties eschew assumptions in favor of facts.

[59] Can be betty in the kitchen; here it's not.

[60] The Beatles are betty. Paul McCartney is a big betty. For a further elucidation of this point, see pages 172–76.

[61] The larger scheme of things is what betties create, but they don't dwell on it.

[62] See "opinions," note 31.

[63] NBC.

cut costs—and *compose* your *epistles*. As you place them in their *envelopes,* you add a *newspaper clipping* where *appropriate.* It's a *habit* you picked up from your *grandmother,* who always kept a *folder* of *interesting clippings* on her *desk.* You think it's a *nice* way to take an *interest* in *the world* and to *share* it with others.

Having *finished* your *personal correspondence,* you pay the *bills* that came in the *mail* the day before. It gives you nightmares[64] to think of ever being delinquent. You include *a personal note* to your *tailor,* telling her how much you like the *window treatments* and *swags* she *custom made* for you. You *write* down *your telephone number,* BEtty 5-4321, and remind her to call as soon as the *slipcover* for your *ottoman* is *finished.*

Now it's *nine o'clock,* the hour when you can *politely* begin to make personal[65] *phone calls.* You would like to speak to *several* of your *friends,* but it would be awkward to call them on *your birthday,* when they should be calling you. Instead, you decide to go *vote.* It was so *nice* of a representative of the *League of Women Voters* to call yesterday to *remind* you about the *election, not that you would have forgotten* anyway, but on *principle* it was a *thoughtful* thing to do. You are almost *ready* to leave your *apartment* when you *notice* markings that look suspiciously like fingerprints on your *picture window.* Because of your *familiarity* with *standard police procedures,* which you have *garnered* over the years from your *careful reading* of *Agatha Christie novels* and your *devotion* to *Court TV,* you know enough not to disturb this *evidence.* This is hard.[66] Your urge to reach for the *window cleaner* is strong. But what if one of the escaped convicts just happened to place his hand on your window as he passed by, and you alone are in *possession* of the missing *link* that could *crack the case?* The thought of dangerous men being anywhere near you gives you *the heebie-jeebies* again. To calm yourself, you quickly *Scotchgard* a *chair* that you just had *reupholstered.* Just as you *finish,* the *phone rings.* The caller asks, "How would you like to keep a *diary* of *your television viewing habits* for *the Nielson* organization?" "Do *socks* need *darning?*" is your *witty reply!* You *cheerfully* accept this *mission* and *inquire* to whom you can write *a thank-you*

[64]Nightmares could be construed as betty, because in order to have a nightmare, one has to have an awareness of good and bad, right and wrong, pleasant and unpleasant. But that's stretching the point, which isn't betty at all.

[65]See "opinions," note 31.

[66]NBC.

note. Oddly, they don't seem to know what you're talking about. You'll get the *address* from *the telephone directory.*

On your way to *the polling place,* you go by *the local card 'n gift shop* to see if anything new came in since yesterday. You are rewarded when you spot a new *bridal magazine* that *lists* all the *caterers* in your area, not to mention a new *shelter magazine featuring* the latest in *interior designs* from *Sweden.* Along with these, you *purchase* two packs of *sugarless gum.* You think about buying *a lottery ticket,* but you just can't bring yourself to spend your *money* that way, even though the one time you did buy a ticket you won eighty *dollars,* which you immediately spent on several *antique teacups* to add to your *collection.* At first it bothered you to *collect* odd pieces rather than buying *a matching set,* but then you realized that your *collection constitutes* a set[67] in its own way! You *reflect* how much in life *depends* on how you look at things.

After doing your *civic duty* and pulling the *levers* on *the voting machine,* your next stop is the *supermarket.* On your way there, you pass the *annual Firemen's Memorial Parade.* The way those *bagpipers* play *"Amazing Grace"* brings tears[68] to your eyes. You go directly to the *Stouffer's* section at the back of the *store* and place *your favorites* in your *shopping cart: Welsh rarebit,* which you *serve* over *white toast points: macaroni and cheese;* and *best* of all, the *scrumpdidliumpcious spinach soufflé.* Since it's *your birthday,* you *decide* it's all right[69]—*just this once!*—to buy yourself a frozen *Sara Lee coconut cake. What the hey,* you can *diet* tomorrow! At *the checkout counter,* you *read* the *covers* of the *magazines.* Both *Women's Day* and *Ladies' Home Journal* look interesting[70] this month, and you add them to your *purchases.* You pack your *grocery bags* yourself, in such a way that you can easily unpack them at home. *Planning, planning, planning.* If you were asked for one word that would best[71] describe *your philosophy of life,* that would have to be it.

The *mailman* is just *finishing* his *sorting* when you arrive *home.* You are excited to find four new *catalogs* that you have never *received* before, as well as *several birthday cards.* Isn't that *nice?* Your *loved ones remembered!* You

---

[67]A set—NBC.

[68]NBC, when it happens to a dress.

[69]*Right* has an NBC when it describes a certain brand of rigid politics that do not reflect the generosity, compassion, and determination for everyone to have nice homes and sweaters and fun that characterize the typical betty.

[70]Betties often use this word to describe things that they find off-putting.

[71]Betties prefer the bettiest. The best can leave out too many of their loved ones.

put your food away, light the *Duraflame log* in *the fireplace,* and settle on the *sofa* to *read.* There's *an article* in one of the *magazines* on how to *schedule* your *time,* which *reminds* you of *your favorite moment* in *literature,* that moving scene *toward* the end of *The Great Gatsby* when Nick Carraway reads *Gatsby's Schedule and General Resolves,* written in his *notebook* on September 12, 1906. When your first read *Gatsby's self-improvement plan,* tears of relief came to your eyes as you recognized *a kindred spirit.* You *wholeheartedly agree* with Gatsby's father; a boy like that was bound[72] to get ahead.

Well! All that *reading* has made you antsy, so you *decide* to do a few *ballet* stretches to work out the kinks. As you are *gathering* up your *leotard* and *ballet slippers,* your *doorbell rings.* It must be that *nice UPS* man with a *birthday* package[73] for you. Or maybe it's the *florist!* Or maybe your *godmother* has *decided* to pay you a spontaneous[74] *visit. Excitedly,* you open the door, only to discover it's *none of the above.* To your surprise, you find three strange men on your *doorstep.*

"How can I help you?" you ask.

"Our car broke down," says the tallest of the men. *"May* we use your *telephone?"*

"Of course!" you say *kindly.* You yourself had *car trouble* once, so you *empathize* with their *predicament.* "But would you *please* wipe your feet on the *doormat* before entering?"[75]

As you lead them *toward* the *telephone,* you *notice* how relieved the men appear to be that you have *invited* them inside. You guess[76] that some of your *neighbors* haven't been quite as *forthcoming* with *help* as you have. You don't blame them but *prefer* to *think the best* of people—as you would have people think the best of you.

"May I offer you *a glass of water?"* you ask. Once inside your house, these men are guests, even if uninvited.

"Do you have any bourbon?" asks one of the men.

You *giggle politely.* "Oh, right," you say, *"as if* anyone would really drink bourbon in the middle of the day! That's a real *knee-slapper!"*

They *exchange* glances and sidle over to the *telephone.* As they make their

[72]NBC.
[73]NBC.
[74]God forbid.
[75]NBC.
[76]*Oi vay.*

call, you *pour* them each *a tall, frosted glass* of *springwater* and then arrange *an array* of Pepperidge Farm *cookies* from their *taste-tempting Seville Collection* on a *plate.* When you return to your *living room,* your *guests* are busy *admiring* your *great-grandmother's silver service* and your set of *Norman Rockwell prints.*

"*Snacks* are *served* in the *dining car!*" you call out *merrily.* You hand them each a glass, a *cocktail napkin,* and a *coaster.* "So what did they say at the garage?"[77]

The men *exchange* glances again. They seem very dependent on each other's reactions. You find it touching to see men who appear to be so close.

"They can't come until tomorrow," says the large man with the scar down the left[78] side of his face.

"*Oh, that's too bad!* What are you going to do?"

"We *thought* maybe we could stay here," says the third man, who appears to be holding a large *whittling* knife.

His *suggestion* throws you into a turmoil. You'd like to *help,* but you only have one extra *bed,* not to *mention* the *fact* that you'd *hoped* to spend the *evening* alone with your *boyfriend.* As you are *debating,* the *doorbell chimes* again. You are *surprised* to see *several* burly *policemen* at your door.

"And *what may I do for you, gentlemen?*" you ask.

"Your *neighbors* said they saw the escaped convicts come in here," *replies* the oldest one.

"*Good heavens,*" you *exclaim.* "What incredible imaginations people have around here! No one has come[79] by except three poor men whose car broke down."

"*Mind* if we come in and take a look?"

"No, *of course* not," you say, although you're not sure you have *enough* cold *springwater* left to go around. You lead the *police* to the *living room,* only to find the men have disappeared! Immediately you *notice* that one of them has left his glass on the *coffee table,* where it is already making a *ring.* "Is there a back way out of here?" ask the *police.*

You point through the *kitchen* as you try to *absorb* the stain with a *sponge.* It doesn't *completely* come up, but that's *all right* because you were going to *re-*

[77]See "opinions," note 31.
[78]See *right,* note 69.
[79]NBC.

finish this *piece of furniture* anyway. You sit back down on the *sofa* to *wait* for either the *police* or the three men to come back. The room is *nice* and *toasty* now from the fire, and you lay your head on a *pillow* and pull your *afghan* up over your *shoulders*. Now you're *good* and *comfy! The next thing you know,* you feel something *soft* on your cheek. It's your *boyfriend,* giving you *little butterfly kisses* to wake you up.

"*Oh,* I *must* have drifted off!" you say. Even though you *know better,* you still think there's something slightly *unacceptable* about taking a *nap* in the *middle* of the *afternoon,* and you hate to be caught doing it.

"I came over *early,*" he says. "I didn't *think* you *should* be alone with those escaped convicts around, but on my way over I heard on the *radio* that they've been caught!"

"*Thank goodness,*" you say. "I just *hope* they aren't *treated* too harshly."

"Speaking of *treated,*" he says, "how about getting ready to go out for *your birthday dinner?*"

He's so *considerate!* You keep an image of his *cute* face in your *mind* the whole *time* you are taking *your second shower of the day,* and you can't help *thinking* that *Frank Capra* was right; *it is a wonderful life!*

Betties Have Hobbies!

Betties are never at a loss for things to do. Whenever they feel the slightest stirrings of the distasteful mood that others call ennui, they immediately go to the bulletin board in the kitchen and check the list of suggested activities posted there. Who could spend an idle afternoon when faced with any of these tempting choices?

antiquing

apple polishing

baking

barbecues

bookbinding

cataloging

comparison shopping

cooking class

copyediting

coupon clipping

darning

decoupage

Easter egg hunts

foreign-language get-togethers

gardening

grouting and regrouting

hand laundering and starching

handicrafts

host(ess)ing

Japanese tea ceremonies

making a list, checking it twice

marinading

origami

pedicures

pet grooming

proofreading

quilting bees

raising bees

reading old issues of *The New Yorker* or *National Geographic*

redecorating

Scotchgarding

silver polishing

singing 'round the campfire

spelling bees

touching up paint chips

Tupperware parties

viticulture

writing thank-you notes

And if all else fails, *thinking* can be a betty activity, depending, of course, on the content of one's thoughts!

Betties Play Sports

And they're darned good sports, too. They're the folks who sincerely believe that it's not whether you win or lose, it's how you play the game. The values of fair play, good sportsmanship, and evenly matched opponents are all betty. Cheating? *Qu'est-ce que c'est?* If you need a person to referee or man the stopwatches or sit on a little chair with her hand on a tennis net, get a betty. Her presence will guarantee that, no matter how fierce the competition, everyone will part as friends.

Play Ball—
Betty's Favorite Sports

speed-walking

miniature golf

ice-skating

tennis

Kadima

volleyball

badminton

horseshoes/quoits

boules/bocci

synchronized swimming

softball

Ping-Pong/table tennis

croquet

dressage

kite-flying

water polo

sailing

skiing

waterskiing

canoeing

kayaking

archery

sheepdog trials

fencing

gymnastics

Betty Sports Stars

Greg Louganis

Cal Ripken

Chris Evert

Pete Sampras

Wayne Gretzky

Scott Hamilton

Mary Lou Retton

Roosevelt Greer

Jack Nicklaus

Dorothy Hamill

Arnold Palmer

Orel Hershiser

Lou Gehrig

Peggy Fleming

Betties Go Out to Dinner

Though you have often heard horrible stories from friends who have worked in restaurants about the sanitary conditions of their kitchens, like most betties, you occasionally enjoy dining at a fine restaurant. (You never say "eating out.") Since betties don't like surprises when it comes to food, you are not likely to be adventurous in your dining habits—which rules out many foreign cuisines, particularly those that require you to sit on the floor and eat with your fingers. You prefer restaurants recommended by friends or written up in newspaper reviews and particularly like books on restaurants that describe the ambience, recommend dishes, and, best of all, reproduce actual menus.

Once a restaurant has been chosen, the true betty will always make a reservation, even if it isn't necessary. Nothing beats the secure feeling of announcing one's name to the maître d', then watching as he runs his finger down the columns in the reservation book and says, "Betty? Yes, a party of four!" Being part of "a party of four" adds a festive air to the evening.

When shown to your table, you will often ask, politely and discretely, to be seated somewhere else. You do not like being too close to the noisy Scylla of the kitchen or the whirling Charybdis-like drafts of the front door. Other potential seating hazards include being placed near smokers or parents accompanied by small children. You may or may not slip the maître d' a little something extra for acceding to your request. If you do, make sure the bill is crisp and clean. This is a way to let the establishment know they're dealing with a discerning customer, and that they should be on their best behavior.

You do not approve of waiters and waitresses who introduce themselves by name ("Hello, I'm Steve, and I'll be your waiter tonight"), but you will use the name, if need be, once you know it, and you will get over your squeamishness at their overfamiliarity when they begin to announce the specials. The betty listens politely to every "special" offering even if she routinely orders exactly the same dish and has no intention of sampling something new. But there are betties who are willing to take a chance on a special (you just love the word), at least as an appetizer. Choosing a special makes you feel adventurous, knowledgeable, and, of course, special, as if the dish had been created just for you.

Reading the menu is the best part of the dining experience for a betty. You

typically have trouble making up your mind and are always the last one at the table to order. "You go first," you say. "There are so many wonderful things, I can't make up my mind." You are very interested in what the people at the next table are eating ("I wonder what it is, it looks so good") and though you may muster the courage to ask them how they like it, you'd die a thousand deaths if they caught you staring.

Once all necessary changes have been made in your order, including the last-minute switch you inevitably make in your choice of salad dressing, it's time to sit back, relax, and listen in on conversations at the nearby tables. Normally, you don't approve of eavesdropping, but you consider conversations that take place in a public venue to be, well, public. Betties particularly like "overhearing" arguments—not the yelling and screaming kind, but the through-clenched-teeth variety. On the way home you will try to discuss the conversations you overheard, only to find out that your dinner companions didn't even notice the man with the pencil-thin mustache old enough to be that young blonde's father or the amount of food consumed by the obese family of four behind you. Wow, it can really be lonely to be so observant.

Dinner itself, when it finally arrives, is most often a disappointment. There's not a dish on this earth that can match the anticipation you felt when reading the menu and deciding what to order. Besides, you believe you could make the entire meal better at home, and, knowing that, it hurts to spend the money on something that will go in one end and out the other. (You don't want to think about *that* at dinner, but you can't help it. You are a betty, after all!)

When the food arrives, more often than not, everyone else appears to have made better choices than you have, and you glance longingly at their plates. If offered a "bite" (yippie!), and if it looks reasonably safe (sanitary considerations are, as always, a consideration), you will taste it politely and praise the dish, no matter what you may privately think of it, as if it reflects on your companion in some essential way. You'd rather hurt your own taste buds than anyone else's feelings.

As the meal progresses, the betty feels yet another tug of ambivalence. While you are against wasting food, you know it is considered indelicate to finish everything on your plate. If you have a dog, or can bluff one, you can always ask for a doggie bag; if not, you must determine the size of the portion you will decline to eat, an amount that will seem neither too wasteful nor too small. You arrange these leftovers carefully on your plate in a pattern that

will create an impression of civilized restraint in the dining room while causing no offense in the kitchen. If the occasion is a particularly lighthearted one, perhaps you will use these leftovers to create a smiling face or the man in the moon. There's no better way to let your waiter know he's doing a good job. (Tip: olives make great eyes!) You may feel slightly guilty about "playing with your food," something your mother warned you never to do, but what is cooking and food presentation but playing with food? Besides, a touch of whimsy and a splash of style are valid excuses for occasionally forsaking edicts primarily intended for children.

Dessert is another high point of the meal and though you couldn't possibly eat another bite, you don't want to ruin anyone else's fun by not ordering one. Choosing from a dessert tray is a particular pleasure, though you always wonder how long those desserts have been left out at room temperature and secretly fear that you will be served one of them, rather than a replica from the refrigerator in the back. Unlike the main course, dessert is rarely a disappointment to you and you clean your plate every time, having heard nothing about indelicacy regarding this.

After ordering a frothy cup of cappuccino—or herbal tea—you catch Steve-the-waiter's eye and he brings you your bill. While you are sipping your beverage, you figure out how much each person at the table owes, including tax and tip. You always do this even if one person is treating (a word betties love to use almost enough to overcome their tendency toward thriftiness—what greater pleasure could there be in life than to stand up and announce, "I'll be treating tonight"?). Finally, Steve takes the check and you thank him for the lovely meal. On your way out, you pick up a handful of after-dinner mints and the restaurant's card. You thank the maître d', telling him you can't wait to get to your desk to record all the details of the evening in your restaurant notebook.

Betties Listen to Music
—Even Rock and Roll!

At first glance, it might not seem that rock and roll has anything in common with bettiness. The image of Ozzy Osbourne biting the head off a rat, Iggy Pop ripping his shirt open with his drumsticks, or Alice Cooper entwined with a snake is enough to make even the most freedom-minded soul wonder if Tipper Gore might have a point with her betty warning labels. But that extreme manner of *épatering la bettoisie* is not the whole picture, thank goodness! There are rockers who have a betty sensibility. Think of Rod Stewart's "Tonight's the Night," in which he exhorted his virgin child to let her *inhibitions* run wild. Yes! Or consider how Joni Mitchell summed up how even betties get the blues in her song "My Old Man," when she characterized her lonesomeness by noticing that in her lover's absence the bed had become too big and the frying pan too wide. And how much more moving can one get than Paul Simon did when he penned the lyrics that celebrated the wonderful friendship between two characters named Betty and Al. When Al gives Betty permission to call him by his nickname, you just know it's the beginning of a beautiful relationship. And the way Paul sings the name "Betty" is enough to make betties everywhere die of pride.

And let's not forget the bettiful lyrics sung by Richard Harris in his rasping, deeply felt version of the Jimmy Webb ballad, "MacArthur Park." When someone leaves the cake out in the rain, and he doesn't think that he can take it, because it took so long to bake it . . . Well. Pick up your handkerchiefs. Who can't identify with that kind of heartbreak?

Here are a few more performers whose musical careers are cloaked in an aura of bettiness.

Amy Grant

Barry Manilow

Neil Diamond

Hootie and the Blowfish

The Captain and Tennille

The Carpenters

Olivia Newton-John

The Monkees

Pat Boone

Bobby Rydell

Abba

But who's the biggest bass-playing betty of them all? I, Elizabeth "Betty" Albright, have a strong opinion on this subject, and on the following pages, I'll make my case. . . .

Dead, or Just Terminally Betty?

A Rumor Exhumed

The following is a never-before-printed interview with the three living Beatles and the widow of John Lennon, Yoko Ono, on a subject they're discussing publicly for the very first time. I'm tickled pink to be able to present these revelations here.

The Abbey Road Studios, where the Beatles were gathered to promote their Anthology CDs, were abuzz with activity when I arrived. Outside on the sidewalk stood a gaggle of the famous Apple Scruffs, the hard-core Beatle birds who hang about in hopes of catching a glimpse of their idols as they enter/exit the building. The birds are a bit long in the tooth these days; those microminis don't look quite as smashing on forty-five-year-olds as they did on girls of fifteen. I'm glad I'm dressed in a sensible pantsuit!

The lads are in the control room, fiddling with instruments and trading jokes. They are just the way I've always pictured them. As I'm setting up my tape recorder, Yoko comes in and begins to spray-paint graffiti on the walls. At first we're all put off, but then we read her message. PAUL IS A BETTY, she has written, and everyone nods. It's a perfect segue into the interview. We all pull up our chairs around a table laden with fresh fruit, carafes of springwater, and bottles of Geritol. I flip open my reporter's notebook, in which I've written my questions, and suddenly my stomach ties up in knots as I realize I'm in the presence of the most famous rock and roll band in history! I counsel myself to count to ten and breathe deeply. Paul gives me a friendly wink that affords me the courage I need. He's so cute!

BETTY ALBRIGHT (hereafter known as B.A.): Thank you, guys, so much for agreeing to this interview. It was really sweet of you.

PAUL: The pleasure is ours, Betty.

B.A.: I wanted to talk about the old myths and rumors about certain subliminal messages on your records. My theory is that all along you were proclaiming that Paul was a betty, not that he was deceased. Am I correct in thinking that?

GEORGE (*chortling*): You caught us, Betty! You're like one of those supergirl

sleuths, like Nancy Drew, or someone like that. The clues have been there since *Meet the Beatles,* but you're the first person who's gotten it. "Paul is dead!" Such morbid bullocks!

B.A.: *Meet the Beatles* . . . Now, correct me if I'm wrong, but isn't the clue there that on the front cover, Paul's head is directly beneath the words "phenomenal Pop," indicating his early goal of becoming a good father?[80]

RINGO: That's it, Betty.

B.A.: And on *The Beatles' Second Album,* in the bottom row of pictures on the front cover, Paul's head is positioned directly below the letters L-E-S on Ringo's bass drum.

YOKO (giggling): L-E-S for LESTOIL!

B.A.: That's what I thought.

RINGO: Let me tell you about one John invented. On the album cover of *Beatles '65,* if you draw a line at a forty-five-degree angle from the tip of Paul's umbrella through the red and black letters in the title of the album, you'll see, in sequence, these letters: N (John), E (Beatles), R (Rock), D (Everybody's). John loved to tease Paul!

PAUL: But I got him back in that case by making my own statement with the broom. See how I'm holding it out, as if I'm offering it to everyone out there in Beatleland? I think by doing that, I actually took control of the situation in a fairly cool way.

B.A.: I thought that's what you were doing!

PAUL: Yeah, well. You were right.

B.A.: Jeeze Louise, it's so great to have you confirm all this for me. For a while, I almost thought I was going crazy when I was noticing all this. Not really, of course. Going crazy is just an expression. Anyway. Anyway, let's talk about *Sgt. Pepper,* which, as you probably know, contains many of the clues that were used in the "Paul is dead" hysteria. Or should I say hoax?

YOKO (giggling): Hoax, hoax!

PAUL: In all fairness, you could call it that. I mean, we knew what we were doing. I remember when I thought the whole thing up. I was riding in the back of a cab with Mick Jagger, Keith Richards, Cliff Richard, Little Richard, Elvis, Bob Dylan, and a few others, and I just said out of the blue, "Why not plant some clues on our albums that will reveal a secret we won't

[80]Sure enough, he has four children and is rumored to be devoted to them all.

betty
AT PLAY

tell anywhere else?" Everyone loved the idea. When I brought it back to the boys, they wanted to do it. And we have kept it a secret all these years. Whenever I see any of those guys, they're still liable to hazard a guess as to what we did. It's actually kind of an interesting social phenomenon, don't you think?

B.A.: Indeed I do!

PAUL: Yeah. Well, here's a document that might interest you. It's my original words to "A Day in the Life," which I wrote one morning as I was waiting to see the dentist. Here, take a look.

With trembling hands, I reach for the document and begin to read.

woke up in an excellent mood after eight solid hours of sleep

popped out of my bed and immediately made it—hospital corners are child's play to me

bent forward from the waist and combed my hair carefully across my head for a stimulating one hundred strokes

walked downstairs at a moderate pace, taking care to hold firmly to the banister, with the caveat in mind that most accidents happen in the home

had a well-balanced breakfast, the foundation of a productive day, and felt good about myself as I sipped a cup of hot chocolate

looking up at my well-oiled grandfather clock, i noticed that i was, as usual, right on schedule

took precautions against infection by bundling up in my coat and hat—i haven't had a cold in years!

arrived at the bus stop in time to greet my neighbors for a few seconds in front of their flat before the bus pulled up

found a comfortable window seat upstairs where I'd be sure to have a nice view of loverly Liverpool

had a nice conversation with an attractive older person who spoke about a recent dream, after which I spent the rest of the ride thinking

about all the things I wanted to accomplish that day

ah . . . ah ah ah . . . ah ah ah . . . ah ah ah . . . ah . . . ah ah ah . . . ah
ah ah . . . ah ah ah . . . ah ah ah ah ah

B.A.: Well, I can see there is certainly a difference in mood between these lyrics and the words of the song the whole world knows and loves. What was John's reaction when he first saw these lyrics?

RINGO: I remember. He took one look at it and said "What the bloody hell? Rewrite this or take your bloody, grotty wings and fly away."

GEORGE: Yeah, and then Paul said, "You're joking." "Nope," said John. Paul said he honestly didn't see what was wrong, except perhaps for a few rough rhymes. Said he didn't know how to fix it. And John said, "Just imagine you're me in the morning. Think of how I feel when I drag me carcass out of bed and bugger off onto a bus." It was really very good advice, when you think of it.

B.A.: And, Paul, you took it, I take it.

PAUL: Oh, yeah, I ran with that. I just needed an angle, you know.

B.A.: What about all those words everyone heard when they played their records backward?

GEORGE: Well, Betty, I don't think we really need to tell you, but we'll go through it anyway, for the record. In "Revolution, #9" we never said, "Turn me on, dead man, turn me on, turn me on." Why would we? What we really said was "Tour me homestead, ma'am, tour me home, tour me home," which was a secret invitation to the queen to come over for a cuppa any time she felt the need.

RINGO: And on "Strawberry Fields," we're saying "cranberry sauce," not "I buried Paul." I mean, if it had come to that, we'd have cremated him anyway.

YOKO: I thought of that.

B.A.: Our time is nearly up, so let me just quickly run through a few other clues.

PAUL: Be our guest, Betty.

B.A.: On *Sgt. Pepper* . . .

GEORGE: Ah, yes. The clues there are the OPB badge on Paul's arm, meaning Officially Pronounced Betty; the yellow flowers forming the bass guitar; Steven Crane pasting down Paul's cowlick; the doll holding the muddy gar-

The betty AT PLAY

175

dening glove; and the way Paul points to the line "Wednesday morning at five o'clock," which shows he gets up early, like all big betties do.

YOKO: He was never cool. John was cool.

RINGO: And on *Magical Mystery Tour,* we had John sit behind a sign that said "I WASH," but then the bloody art director squeezed it between the desk caddy and the pen stand and so you can't see the H anymore.

PAUL: And on *Abbey Road,* when I'm barefoot and holding a cigarette? I'm really carrying the piece of chalk I used to make notes during our recording sessions, and I'm barefoot 'cuz I just sent me Beatle boots out to the repair shop.

B.A.: Just as I thought. Boys, this has been most enlightening, not to mention informative, fun, and, I must admit, somewhat of a personal victory for me.

GEORGE: We're glad to have it all off our chests.

RINGO: We're grateful to *you.*

Just before I left the room, Yoko nodded her head slightly in my direction, as if to say she approved of what had transpired between all of us during the past half hour, and I felt ten feet tall. It was wonderful to meet the Fabs and journalistically satisfying to lay an old rumor to rest. I understood how Geraldo Rivera must have felt as he approached Al Capone's cellar. Except I was even luckier—I got the goods! Of course, it would have been nice if the truth had come out at the time and no one would ever have had to fear that Paul was dead. But bettier late than never!

The Top 100 Betty Rock and Roll Song Titles

The following titles demonstrate that Paul is in good company:

SONG	ARTIST
A Question of Temperature	The Balloon Farm
A Whiter Shade of Pale	Procol Harum
Be True to Your School	The Beach Boys
Beauty Is Only Skin Deep	The Temptations
Beware of Darkness	George Harrison
Bread and Butter	The Newbeats
Breaking Up Is Hard to Do	Neil Sedaka
Brown Sugar	The Rolling Stones
Build Me Up, Buttercup	The Foundations
Chain Letter	Todd Rundgren
Cole Slaw	Frank Culley
Crimson and Clover	Tommy James and the Shondelles
Daddy's Home	Shep and the Limelights
Darlin' Be Home Soon	The Lovin' Spoonful
Ding Dong, Ding Dong	George Harrison
Don't Let the Sun Catch You Crying	Gerry and the Pacemakers
Feeling Alright?	Traffic
Fixing a Hole	The Beatles
Get a Job	The Silhouettes
Give Peace a Chance	John Lennon
Glycerine	Bush
God Save the Queen	The Sex Pistols
Golden Slumbers	The Beatles
Good Vibrations	The Beach Boys
Handy Man	Jimmy Jones
Have You Ever Been Mellow?	Olivia Newton-John
Here Comes the Sun	The Beatles
Holiday	Madonna
Hope You're Feeling Better	Santana
I Hear a Symphony	The Supremes
I Can See Clearly Now	Johnny Nash
I Must Not Think Bad Thoughts	X

SONG	ARTIST
I Can Help	Billy Swan
I Love My Mom	The Roches
I Believe in Music	Gallery
I'd Like to Teach the World to Sing	The New Seekers
I'm a Believer	The Monkees
If You Can't Say Something Nice	Roy Orbison
If I Had a Hammer	Peter, Paul and Mary
In My Diary	The Moonglows
Incense and Peppermints	Strawberry Alarm Clock
It's My Party	Leslie Gore
Knock Three Times	Dawn
La Isla Bonita	Madonna
Let Me Sleep on It	Meat Loaf
Little Red Corvette	Prince and the Revolution
Lollipop	The Chordettes
Look at Your Hands	George Michael
Love Will Keep Us Together	Captain and Tennille
Mother-in-Law	Ernie-K-Doe
Mr. Pharmacist	The Other Half
Mrs. Brown, You've Got a Lovely Daughter	Herman's Hermits
My Best Friend	The Jefferson Airplane
My Hometown	Bruce Springsteen
Nights in White Satin	The Moody Blues
Oh Gee, Oh Gosh	The Kodoks
Our House	Crosby, Stills, Nash and Young
Peanut Butter	The Marathons
Perfect World	Talking Heads
Please Mr. Postman	The Marvelettes
Positive Vibration	Bob Marley and the Wailers
Reach Out of the Darkness	Friend and Lover
Respect	Otis Redding
Respect Yourself	Staple Singers
Return to Sender	Elvis Presley
Rikki Don't Lose That Number	Steely Dan
Rockin' Chair	The Band
See You Later, Alligator	Bill Haley and His Comets
Separate Beds	Squeeze

SONG	ARTIST
Shop Around	Smoky Robinson and the Miracles
Smells Like Teen Spirit	Nirvana
Solitaire	The Embers
Son of a Preacher Man	Dusty Springfield
Stairway to Heaven	Led Zeppelin
Sweet Home Alabama	Lynyrd Skynyrd
Synchronicity	The Police
Take Good Care of My Baby	Bobby Vee
Teddy Bear	Elvis Presley
Tell It Like It Is	Aaron Neville
Tell the Truth	Ray Charles
The Clean-Up Woman	Betty Everett
The Sun Is a Very Magic Fellow	Donovan
The Little Old Lady (from Pasadena)	Jan and Dean
These Boots Are Made for Walking	Nancy Sinatra
Tie a Yellow Ribbon 'Round the Old Oak Tree	Tony Orlando and Dawn
Tutti-Frutti	Little Richard
Uncle Albert/Admiral Halsey	Paul and Linda McCartney
Wake Up Little Susie	The Everly Brothers
Walk Like a Man	The Four Seasons
Walk—Don't Run	The Ventures
Waterwheel	Hall and Oates
What's So Funny about Peace Love and Understanding?	Nick Lowe
White Room	Cream
Who'll Stop the Rain?	Creedence Clearwater Revival
Wouldn't It Be Nice?	The Beach Boys
You Can't Judge a Book by Its Cover	Bo Diddley
You Can Make It If You Try	Sly and the Family Stone
You Can't Always Get What You Want	The Rolling Stones
Your Mother Should Know	The Beatles
Yummy Yummy Yummy	Ohio Express

Just When You Thought It Was Safe . . .

Though I'd like to continue this discussion of fun forever, there's another topic waiting in the wings, a dastardly subject that's liable to pop out and ruin everything if I don't deal with it soon. So brace yourselves and, please, don't read this next section when you're alone in the house or late at night. It isn't going to be pretty.

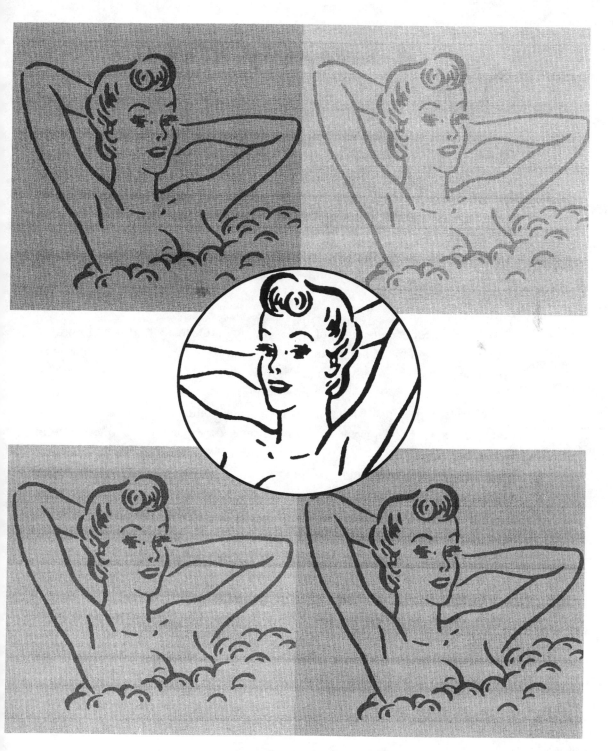

the antibetty

A Slippery Slope

You've just arrived home from a trip to Atlantic City. You parked your car next to a fire hydrant, you let the dog out to roam the neighborhood without supervision, your suitcase is full of dirty laundry. You're exhausted. Every muscle in your body hurts. All you want to do is to flop down on the sofa, chug a few brewskies, order a pizza, and watch a little *Married with Children*. You feel guilty about the prospect of having such an unseemly evening, but what the hell, you deserve to cut loose once in a while. After all, who will ever know?

Tsk, tsk, tsk. Betty, Betty, Betty. Pull yourself together fast! This is exactly the type of instance when you have to be most vigilant. If everybody just let things go whenever they felt tired, what do you think would happen to the world?

Go find a proper parking spot, put your dog on a leash and take him for a decent walk, and make a nice and easy vegetable stir-fry. And why not pour it over a bed of nutritious brown rice? Surely you have some in your freezer that you could heat up quickly in the microwave!

Civilization begins at home. If you let your home go, even for a moment, don't be surprised when you hear about revolutions or civil disobedience in the outside world. As to who would ever know if you let yourself go to pieces, *YOU* would know. A seemingly innocent pizza on the sofa one day has been known to lead to a bottle of Ripple and a handful of pork rinds in the basement the next. At that point, antibettiness is just around the corner, with the apocalypse not far behind.

Yes, Virginia, there is an Antibetty (not to be confused with Auntie Betty). Some folks would probably prefer to avoid this truth, but betties, who tend to live by aphorisms, know that to be forewarned is to be forearmed. Speaking of which, could your forearms use a bit of toning? The greatest weapon in the struggle against the Antibetty is never to let anything go. Why not pick up a four-pound barbell and do a mini-workout as you read the following? You'll end up smarter *and* stronger! The Antibetty won't like that.

Mr. Hyde

*L*et's take a closer look at some of the ways that antibettiness has seeped into our culture and some of the people who have fallen prey to its temptations so that we may prevent it from permeating any of our own membranes. Remember, the aim is to be the picture of inner perfection, not the picture of Dorian Gray.

Antibetties

Tony Montana

Vlad the Impaler

Ted Kaczynski

Roseanne

Oliver Stone

Dennis Hopper

Ozzy Osbourne

Pigpen

Hell's Angels

R. Crumb

John Belushi

Gary Busey

Roman Polanski

Courtney Love

Antibetty Language

Just as there is a betty vocabulary, there are words and phrases the good betty would do best to avoid. Remember, a tidy vocabulary reflects a tidy brain, not to mention an actual tidy bowl.

absentminded, ad absurdum, angle for, antisocial, bad actor, bad temper, beer and skittles, by fits and starts, charley horse, cut adrift, dark horse, double meaning, extramarital relations, flotsam and jetsam, fly-by-night, fly off the handle, fork over, frame-up, freelance, give the lowdown, go against the grain, hatchet man, helter-skelter, high jinks, high off the hog, hit the bottle, ill at ease, ill repute, ill-usage, in embarrassed circumstances, inferiority complex, kept woman, Mickey Finn, off-color, out-of-the-way, pell-mell, rabble-rouser, red-handed, reductio ad absurdum, shelf-worn, shifty, sidestep, skimble-skamble, soft soap, speakeasy, spread-eagle, stool pigeon, topsy-turvy, turn one's stomach, upside down, whipping boy, wibble-wobble, willy-nilly, witch-hunt.

Antibetty Addresses

Since the first time a Cro-Magnon man deliberately chose a cave with a southern exposure, humans have been concerned with where they live. Betties are no exception. Although they are able to make the best of a bad lot, there are nevertheless limits to what they can do with even the most realistic brick face. These are addresses even the most optimistic betties will do their best to avoid, no offense to the current owners or their authorized representatives.

Tobacco Road

down in the boondocks

Texarkana

Hole in the Wall

the wrong side of the tracks

East of Eden

Sodom

Spahn Ranch

downtown

shantytown

77 Sunset Strip

the dark side of the moon

the House of the Rising Sun

Heartbreak Hotel

Bates Motel

Love Canal

Betties Run Amok

There is a dark side to bettiness that most betties would prefer to sweep out from under the rug and dispose of forever, but for the sake of a thorough examination of the subject, facts must be faced and skeletons in the closet bravely exposed (tastefully shrouded, of course). To state the matter in its baldest, most depilated form, there are cases of betties gone bad. As you read the following list, spend a few minutes thinking about exactly where these poor folks went wrong, so you can prevent such a fate ever befalling you!

Adam and Eve

Claudine Longet

Marilyn Chambers

Dr. Jekyll

Margaret Trudeau

Oliver North

Princess Stephanie

Lizzie Borden

Jean Harris

Leona Helmsley

Drew Barrymore

Marianne Faithful

Alfred Hitchcock

Jean Seberg

Travis Bickle

Imelda Marcos

Yukio Mishima

Benito Mussolini

General William T. Sherman

Howard Hughes

Spalding Gray

Woody Allen

Timothy Leary

Roy Cohn

Boy George

Anita Bryant

Pee-wee Herman

Jesse Helms

Michael Jackson

Rob Lowe

Jan-Michael Vincent

Hugh Grant

Johnny Depp

O. J. Simpson

The anti-betty

187

Recovering Betties

This is a special category of betty who has had an unfortunate experience with drugs or alcohol or both, and who has since come clean about her addiction. Anyone who regularly passes the checkout counters in supermarkets knows that a week cannot go by without one celebrity or another announcing their successful completion of a recovery program. To paraphrase Tolstoy, all big betties are happy, productive individuals, while all addicts are essentially alike. Yet the recovery stories of ex-addicts continue to hold a strange fascination for those who've never had more than their cotton sheets to the wind.

How do they do it? One of the most popular ways is to enter a recovery program at an institution such as—and you knew this was coming—the Betty Ford Center. Betty Ford is the patron saint of many addicts, an inspiration to celebrities such as Liz Taylor, Liza Minnelli, and Johnny Cash. Her program has been a success where other methods have failed, and the basic concepts of the Betty Ford Center have been copied all over the country. So what is her secret? Why, there's no secret at all, unless you still feel hush-hush about bettiness! At the Betty Ford Center, celebrity and noncelebrity alike come to brass tacks by cleaning. Their day is filled from dawn to dusk with chores and activities designed to keep their bodies busy as their minds absorb perky betty epigrams and helpful thoughts. Not only do they make their beds and take out the garbage (even the biggest celebrities are not exempt from these chores!), but they do mental housecleaning to rid themselves of negative thoughts and destructive memories. At the end of four weeks, they emerge into the world scrubbed and refurbished, ready to just say no to all the addictive substances so available at Hollywood parties and on movie sets. If they weren't betties before they went to the recovery center, they are usually betties when they come out; many of them report that they enjoyed making their own beds!

All of this talk of addiction and drugs may sound very far away from the life of the average betty (except those who take bettiness too far—see page 190), but there are lessons to be learned from the Betty Ford Center that can be applied when trying to break any bad habit. Tempted to bite your nails? Take out the garbage! Want another chocolate doughnut? Scrub the toilet! Feel like you can't make an appointment when you know Oprah will be on? Write

a letter to a dead relative forgiving him or her for any past infractions! If you can't go to the Betty Ford Center, make the Betty Ford Center come to you! (No disrespect meant to the great religion of Islam or any of its practitioners.)

Betty Recoverers

Mary Tyler Moore

William Hurt

Chevy Chase

Eileen Brennan

Tony Curtis

Robert Mitchum

Tammy Faye Bakker

Stevie Nicks

Tanya Tucker

Drew Barrymore

James Woods

Kris Kristofferson

Mackenzie Phillips

Lauren Tewes

Papa John Phillips

Don Johnson

Kelsey Grammer

et bettera . . . can you name fifty more?

Betty Overboard!

Yes, there can be too much of a good thing. For certain unfortunates, there is no such thing as betty enough! For them, one set of coasters—or doilies or iced-tea spoons or *anything*—doesn't satisfy. They need them ad infinitum—and, let's face it, infinity isn't betty. Although it's true that tidying tasks are in the deepest sense never done, the normal betty can take a break between attic cleanings or carburetor buffings without too much discomfort.

Not so for the poor betty who becomes addicted to bettiness itself.

To paraphrase the words of Mick Jagger, they cannot procure even a smidgeon of satisfaction from even their most prodigious efforts.

There is help. There is Betties Anonymous (or BA for those in the know, although this is not the BA one wants to acquire). Modeled on Alcoholics Anonymous, this is a twelve-step program designed to afford recovery from excessive bettiness, one Dobie pad at a time. (There is a radical group of recovering betties who've tried for some time to trim the number of steps down to ten, in order to mesh more easily with the coming of the metric system, but the majority view is that these mavericks, while they may have gotten the decimal point, have missed the bigger picture.) Betties Anonymous is a fellowship, which is especially important in the case of this addiction, as one couldn't, shouldn't, wouldn't even want to, give up bettiness altogether, and it is useful to check with others about appropriate parameters. And someone in the group is bound to have a punch bowl with matching cups for all!

Signs That You May Need Betties Anonymous

1. Have you tatted more than ten doilies in the last month *for no good reason?*

2. Do you store your Hallmark cards separately from other brands?

3. Does the concept of "spring cleaning" strike you as reductive?

4. Do you find yourself envying people with pesky lawn problems, and secretly wish you could go back to the summer when you spent your afternoons excising onion grass?

5. Does the sentence "I'm sorry, but you've dialed the wrong number" strike at the core of your self-esteem?

6. Do you think squirrels should be required to wear booties?

7. Have the words "cussed tile grout" ever appeared in your prayers?

8. Have you made more than five public nuisance citizen's arrests in the past year?

9. Are you thrilled at the prospect of a morning spent with a clogged drain?

10. Do you take your personal days when the next issue of *Martha Stewart Living* is due so you can be home to receive it?

If you have answered yes to more than three of the above, get thee to a meeting *au jour d'hui!*

The anti-betty

191

The Twelve Steps of Betties Anonymous

1. We admitted that we were powerless over our bettiness—that our lives had become . . . well, let's just say it wasn't pretty.

2. Came to believe that a betty greater than ourselves could restore us to our original burled sheen, not to mention make us sanitary.

3. Made a decision to turn our will and our other important papers over to the care of the Ubiquitous, Invisible Betty, as we understood her.

4. Made a searching and fearless inventory of our cabinets and drawers.

5. Admitted to the Ubiquitous, Invisible Betty and to another human being the exact measurements of our sarongs.

6. Were entirely ready to have the Ubiquitous, Invisible Betty remove all our defects of character. Duh!

7. Humbly asked her to remove our slipcovers.

8. Made a list (yes! Now we're talking!) of all persons we had harmed and became willing to do mending for them all.

9. Created direct mail campaigns for such people whenever possible, except when to do so would interfere with the routine operations of the United States Postal Service.

10. Continued to take inventory, and when we came across something we hadn't previously registered/warrantied/recorded/insured, we promptly did so.

11. Sought through Bayer Aspirin and betitation to improve our conscious contact with the Ubiquitous, Invisible Betty as we understood her, praying only for knowledge of her laundry secrets.

12. Having had a spiritual awakening as the result of these steps, we got up, made our beds, and broke our fast nutritiously, practicing the principle that breakfast is the most important meal of the day!

A Word about Obsessive-Compulsive Disorder

Obsessive-compulsive disorder (OCD) is an unfortunate syndrome that ruins lives, wastes valuable resources such as water, and often drives the sufferer nuts. It is not a synonym for bettiness, nor do betties have OCD. They are as likely to develop it as they are to come down with any other disease. If they do become victim to it, they are liable to recognize the symptoms quickly from the many women's magazine articles they have read on the subject and seek help early on. With the help of a little Prozac, the betty is soon back on track: a little older, a little wiser, a little more grateful to be committed to the Middle Way than ever before.

Betty Ailments

Betties do have their problems, however. The following are among the most common:

poison oak

dyslexia

vertigo

color blindness

homesickness

sprained ankle

sunburn

migraine

pms

carpal tunnel syndrome

tennis elbow

water on the knee

allergies

palpitations

stress fracture

astigmatism

stage fright

Pus and Pestilence

The Antibetty can give herself away by complaining of any of the following:

herpes

shingles

lice

athlete's foot

scabies

swine flu

goiter

Tourette's syndrome

chlamydia

acne vulgaris

gout

mange

agoraphobia[81]

[81]Although a lot of phobias are very betty, this one, fear of the marketplace, goes too far.

Betty Crimes

Need it be said that criminal activity is anathema to the betty? In general, either they uphold the law, or, if they feel it is unjust, legally work to change it. But, betties being human, lapses have been known to occur. These range in import from major wrongdoings that usually involve computers and accounting and fall under the rubric of white-collar crime to incidences of jaywalking and illegal leaf-burning. Bank robberies, jewelry heists, and even certain murders have their betty aspects due to the degree of planning they require, though of course, by the time one gets around to making such plans, one is a real betty no more.

However, there are other violations perpetrated by actual betties that may not be considered crimes by the public at large but are nevertheless considered quite serious by betties themselves. Read the entries in the crime blotter below for examples of these transgressions.

The Tidy Tattler Tribune Crime Blotter

Sunday 10:09 A.M. Mrs. Willoughby of Rose Lane walked in late to church, then began to cough furiously, distracting the others from their prayers. At the coffee hour after the service, she explained that she had a bad cold and was late because she had stopped at a convenience store to buy an over-the-counter cold remedy. Her fellow parishioners agreed that, rather than risking the infection of the entire congregation, Mrs. Willoughby should have made a different judgment call and just stayed home.

Monday 9:03 A.M. Eager to get to her tennis lesson, Judy Morrow took a dangerous laundry shortcut and put a load into the machine without separating whites from darks. That afternoon she took her ruined polo shirts, tennis

skirts, and underclothes to the dry cleaner, only to be told there was nothing he could do. Now Judy is faced with the choice of throwing out half her wardrobe or putting a brave face on her mistake by pretending she tie-dyed everything on purpose.

Tuesday 4:42 P.M. Bobby Morgan finished the gallon of milk in the family refrigerator and *did not replace it!*

Wednesday 11:18 P.M. Henrietta Spellman remembered it was her sister-in-New Hampshire's birthday when it was too late to call.

Thursday 3:15 P.M. On a rainy day, a group of teenage girls who were going over to a Park Street house for an after-school study date neglected to wipe their feet on the doormat before entering.

Friday 12:00 P.M. Miriam Letters, the town librarian, returned from an evening out with friends right on the stroke of midnight, too late to make a legitimate diary entry for the day.

Saturday 1:10 P.M. Barnes Cadwallader returned library books that were actually due the day before. To add insult to injury, he tried to make an excuse for why he'd been late—something about being the lone survivor of a single-engine-plane crash and having been kept overnight in the hospital for observation—but Miriam Letters gave him such a withering look that he finally lay a dollar on the desk and left without waiting for change.

Although none of these missteps may seem too reprehensible by themselves, each of them is a chink in the dike of civilization. If everyone allowed themselves a similar set of peccadillos, the flood would be upon us again very soon. It is up to each of us to do our part in making the world safe for democracy and all other forms of life.

Remember, prevention is the very bettiest cure of all!

Madcap Betties

These folks are often mistakenly confused with Antibetties, when their true genius is to combine flamboyant personalities with attitudes based on the highest principles of bettiness.

Erma Bombeck

the Galloping Gourmet

Heloise

Julia Child

Barbara Cartland

Richard Simmons

Salvador Dali

Tony Randall

Diane Keaton

Joan Rivers

Willard Scott

Steve Martin

Jim Jay Bullock

Borderline Betties

This is a painful category, in that it contains the names of women who *should*, by all rights, be betties, but whose lives have been a bit too complicated for them to be automatically classified as such.

Jacqueline Onassis

Elizabeth Taylor

Pamela Harriman

Princess Diana

Princess Caroline

Wallis Simpson

Antibetty Seek 'n' Find

Here's a final chance to familiarize yourself with the kinds of things you want to avoid. Find these words in the puzzle on page 201.

abstract
    expressionism

acid rain

acne vulgaris

Al Bundy

all you can eat

apoplexy

asbestos

athlete's foot

barf

Beirut

BO

bulimia

chlamydia

clashing

clodhoppers

crack

devil may care

dildo

dingleberry

free-form

fungus

generic

gin legs

gluttony

golden showers

greasy kid stuff

guzzle

halitosis

hangnail

hangover

head cheese

the heartbreak
    of psoriasis

heavy metal

hunting

jock itch

Judas goat

Las Vegas

Lenny Bruce

malt liquor

marathon

mildew

NAMBLA

nose ring

oil spill

one size fits all

pit stop

plaque

primal scream

Rambo

ring around the collar

rococo

scrapple

shoddy
    workmanship

sinkhole

skinheads

sloth

smegma

snot

sordid

Symbionese

tattoo

Ted Bundy

Texas catheter

the Third World

toxic waste dump

tripe

varicose veins

```
T C G U Z Z L E N A T A S O G C O N E S I Z E F I T S A L L
R H R N G R O S S O U T A S K I N H E A D S A R E E V I L A
I E E A I O X S H O D D Y W O R K M A N S H I P Y T T I H S
N A A H C R A P O R E S D I T E S S N I E V E S O C I R A V
G V S Z E K E I L L I O N O U N C E P R M A N S O N C S U E
A Y Y K L A S S Y S C R U B B E R X H O S E C L A S H I N G
R M K C U R R Y O I L D B E W G A R G C L O S H C R E N U A
O E I U G L Y T A N U I D H O I P O L O I G R A N N A K I S
U T D F R A I Z B U N D E V E N P L U C K B O N E A D H O R
N A S D I L D O A R O O T R L L L O T O A M U G V I C O M O
D L T B A L L I H U E F R A B E E N T R E A P O U J H L S D
T B U H G Y D N U B L A P M X G N E O C I L O V L Y E E I I
H A F S L O T H N O R F K B I S U N N D A T R E G O E O N R
E G F I J U K A T O A R B O T T L E Y Q U L O R A E S N O T
C O O N S C A N I X B E L O F T H M U B M I T U R I E B D O
O L D Q U A R G N I S E O P A P A E L T R Q U O I T S S E X
L S A J O N I N G O O F B A L L S C U M M U U A S S A C H P
L U N O R E A A S I S O L O H C B O R D O O C L A M C L E M
A G I C L A G I B E X R I C H E E T R O A R P E G P I G G U
R N A K I T I L T A P M E A T I S M U I R D R E J O D L I D
B U L I M I A E X P O X M A R A T H O N A S M U D E R R M E
A F A T O O L P O O T T A T U G O J U D A S G O A T A O E I
L A O C E H R O O P S A D A E D S I D O G L I V E N I S O S
B L I H T E R R O L T G O L D E N S H O W E R S F A N B L A
M S L A V E R Y B E I D G U N S A N D R O S E S M I L D E W
A B S T R A C T E X P R E S S I O N I S M I S E R E A T M C
N I P A N D O R A Y R R E B E L G N I D X Y Z A B C P I G I
P R I M A L S C R E A M O S Y M B I O N E S E W A W A I O X
O C L O D H O P P E R S A G O G T E X A S C A T H E T E R C
A L L B O Y E R A C Y A M L I V E D L R D W D R I H T E H T
```

Bettiness Is All

So next time someone asks you to come along for a week-end junket to Las Vegas, remember where a seemingly innocent skip-to-my-lou on the wild side could lead, and just say no!

epilogue

Turn, Turn, Turn
(and we're not talking rotisseries anymore . . .)

In spite of the healthiest of habits and the sanest of lives, the Grim Reaper visits Betty just like everyone else. But the betty is prepared. Betties…

- have insurance policies at least sufficient to cover their funeral expenses, and often enough to pay their grandchildren's way through Bennington, including the requisite dropout year of finding oneself somewhere in Europe.

- work on their wills periodically all their lives, so they're always up-to-date and can never be challenged by disgruntled relatives who are too lazy to go out and make a living on their own. Betties never die intestate. To them, it sounds like a very unpleasant condition to be discussed only in a tête-à-tête with a urologist.

- buy burial plots, or leave explicit cremation instructions.

- choose their own epitaphs, to make sure someone gets it right.

- label everything in their houses with the name of the person who is to keep the item after Betty's death so there will be no unseemly tussles that Betty won't be around to resolve.

- go relatively gently into that good night, at least insofar as anyone would notice. No harrowing deathbed confession scenes for them. (What's to confess? Okay, maybe once Betty wore a hem held up with safety pins. Is this any time to quibble? Betty knows better.)

- rest in peace.

All Goody-Goody Things Must Come to an End . . . or Must They?

As to whatever became of the big betty who was my original inspiration, the last time I saw her she'd become the food services manager at a nice, old hotel in Boston. On the walls of her office were pictures of her husband and children, each stage of their lives appearing happier and more fruitful than the last. Here, I thought, was the essence of all my years of research, and I was pleased to have traveled such a neatly formed circle back to the place I began.

"So, Betty," I said. "The advice you gave me as a child has certainly held true for you. Your name really did set a steady course for your life."

To my surprise, a strange, faraway look came into her eyes. "But my real name isn't Betty," she said quietly.

"What?" I gasped.

"It was Siobhan, but no one could pronounce it when I moved here, so I began calling myself Betty. It made life smoother all around."

"This is a truly astonishing revelation," I said. I was reeling! "You've always been such a betty! I can't imagine you as anything else, to mention nothing of the theory that I've based on you and your name. I don't quite think Siobhan-ness works as well."

"There's no reason for you to change the name of your theory," she said thoughtfully. "You chose well, as did I."

"I suppose," I said, though I was still concerned. "Let me ask you, if you had it to do over, would you still change your name today?"

"I've never thought about it. Now that you ask, I'm not sure. I don't really believe a name can make that much of a difference, but then again, Betty has certainly worked for me. . . ."

Before she could complete her answer, the telephone rang. I watched Betty listen to her caller with the intense yet empathetic concentration that had influenced me so much as a child.

"I'm sorry, we'll have to continue this conversation another time," she said after she hung up. "They need me in the main dining room."

Of course they do, Betty. They always will.

epilogue

205

A Selected Betty Bibliography

(In alphaBETTYcal order, of course!)

Betty Smith Adams. *Dryden's Translation of Vergil and Its Eighteenth-Century Successors.*

Betty Askwith. *A Victorian Young Lady.*

Betty J. Bauml. *A Dictionary of Gestures.*

Honoré de Balzac. *Cousin Betty.*

Betty Billipp. *Please Pass the Salt.*

Betty A. Blue. *Authentic Mexican Cooking.*

Betty Cadbury. *Playthings Past.*

Betty Chamberlain. *The Artist's Guide to His Market.*

Betty Charles. *This Is Your City: London and the Thames.*

Betty Ann Clamp. *Cooking with Low-Cost Proteins.*

Betty Collins. *The Second Step.*

Barnaby Conrad. *Time Is All We Have: Four Weeks at the Betty Ford Center.*

Betty Coon. *Seaward.*

Betty Crocker. *Betty Crocker's Step-by-Step Cookbook.*

Betty Dederich. *I'm Betty D.: Selected Writings.*

Betty Dubanel. *Gare St. Lazare.*

Betty Hanna Elliott. *Doodle Bugs and Cactus Berries.*

Betty Firm. *False Idols.*

Betty Lorraine Fladeland. *Men and Brothers: Anglo-American Antislavery Corporation.*

Betty Flanders Thomson. *The Shaping of America's Heartland: The Landscape of the Middle West.*

Betty S. Flowers. *Browning and the Modern Tradition.*

Betty Ford. *A Glad Awakening.*

Betty Ford. *The Times of My life.*

Betty Grace George. *Education for Africans in Tanganyika.*

Betty Glad. *Jimmy Carter: In Search of the Great White House.*

Roderick Grant. *The Lone Voyage of Betty Mouat.*

Betty Leban Harragan. *Games Mother Never Taught You.*

Robert Goode Hogan. *Betty and the Beast: A Play in Two Acts.*

Betty Jo Tottman Jensen. *From England to America: The Tottman Genealogy.*

Betty Jean Birkholz Joeboans. *Creative Writing in Central Africa.*

Betty Kennedy. *Hurricane Hazel.*

Betty Killingbeck. *Women on Stamps.*

Betty Kushen. *Benjamin Franklin and His Biographers.*

Betty Lee. *Love and Whiskey: The Story of the Dominion Drama Festival.*

Betty Leslie-Melville. *There's a Rhino in the Rosebed, Mother.*

Betty Lewis. *Watsonville: Memories That Linger.*

Betty Lewis. *Watsonville Yesterday.*

Betty Jean Lifton. *Twice Born: Memoirs of an Adopted Daughter.*

Betty-Bright P. Low. *France Views America, 1765–1815.*

Betty L. McCay. *Sources for Genealogical Searching in Philadelphia.*

Betty I. Madden. *Arts, Crafts and Architecture in Early Illinois.*

Betty Reid Mandell, ed. *Welfare in America: Controlling the "Dangerous Classes."*

Betty M. Mann. *The Manns of Edward County, Illinois.*

Betty Massingham. *Turn on the Fountains: A Life of Dean Role.*

Betty Jane Meggers. *Prehistoric America: An Ecological Perspective.*

Betty Anne Miller. *The Cornelius Jensen Family History.*

Hannah More. *Betty Brown, the St. Giles Orange Girl.*

Betty Rose Nagle. *The Poetics of Exile: Program and Polemic in the "Tristila" and "Epistulae ex Ponto" of Ovid.*

Betty B. Osman. *Learning Disabilities: A Family Affair.*

Betty Patterson. *I Reached for the Sky.*

Betty Patterson, ed. *Some Pioneer Families in Wisconsin.*

Betty Lou Phillips. *The Picture Story of Dorothy Hamill.*

Betty Radice. *Who's Who in the Ancient World.*

Betty T. Rahv. *From Sartre to the New Novel.*

Betty Rauers. *Sojourn in Savannah.*

Betty Ring, ed. *Needlework: An Historical Survey.*

Betty Rivera. *Inkstands and Inkwells: A Collector's Guide.*

Betty Wallace Robinette. *Teaching English to Speakers of Other Languages.*

Betty Roland. *The Touch of Silk.*

Betty Root. *Learning to Read: A Catalogue of Books for All Stages and Ages.*

Betty Rosbottom. *Betty Rosbottom's Cooking School Cookbook.*

Betty Ross. *How to Beat the High Cost of Travel.*

Kathryn Morgan Ryan. *The Betty Tree.*

Peter Schikele. *Notebook for Betty-Sue Bach.*

Betty G. Sherman. *American Recipes in English and Spanish.*

Betty Carter McGuire Smoot. *Days in an Old Town.*

Bram Stoker. *Miss Betty.*

Betty Talsedge. *How-to-Cook-a-Pig and Other Back-to-the-Farm Recipes.*

Betty Underwood. *The Forge and the Forest.*

Anthony C. vanKampen. *Betty Smit: Free Lance voor God.*

Doug Warren. *Betty Grable, the Reluctant Movie Queen.*

Betty White. *Betty White in Person.*

Betty Harvey Williams. *Cook's Crier, the Franklin Fireplace.*

Betty Willsher. *Stones: A Guide to Some Remarkable Eighteenth-Century Gravestones.*

Betty Jane Wylie. *Beginnings: A Book for Widows.*

Michiko Yamamoto. *Betty-San.*

Betty H. Zisk. *Local Interest Politics: A One-Way Street.*